A BRETHREN IN CHRIST
WORLD
COOKBOOK

Commissioned by
BRETHREN IN CHRIST WORLD MISSIONS
as part of its centennial celebration

EVANGEL PUBLISHING HOUSE
NAPPANEE   INDIANA

Published by the Board for World Missions
of the Brethren in Christ Church
in cooperation with Evangel Publishing House
Library of Congress Data, etc.

ISBN 0-916-035-83-2
Library of Congress Catalog Number 97-78195

Cookbook Committee
Erma Sider, *Editor*
Kas Bert
Ethel Brubaker
Erma Hoover
Nancy Ives
A J Mann
Eleanor Poe
Ruth Zook

Book and Chapter Introductions
Harriet Bicksler

Design and Layout
Geoff Isley

Photography
Ethel and Graybill Brubaker
George Bundy
George and Marlene Comfort
Graham Guest (Saskatchewan Education)
Trudy McClane
Dick and Ettie Miller
Harvey Sider
Miriam Wenger

Approximate Metric Equivalents

SMALL LIQUID AND DRY MEASURES

1/4 teaspoon	1 mL
1/2 teaspoon	2 mL
1 teaspoon	5 mL
1 tablespoon	15 mL
1 coffee measure	25 mL

LIQUID MEASURE

1 fl oz	30 mL
2 fl oz	60 mL
3 fl oz	100 mL
4 fl oz	125 mL
6 fl oz	200 mL
8 fl oz	250 mL

DRY MEASURE

1/4 cup	50 mL
1/2 cup	125 mL
1 cup	250 mL
2 cups	500 mL
4 cups	1 liter

ABBREVIATIONS

for measurements used throughout the book

cup	c.
gallon	gal.
pint	pt.
pound	lb.
quart	qt.
tablespoon	T.
teaspoon	t.

We acknowledge...
Our donors: Brethren in Christ cooks, photographers and story tellers from each country where Brethren in Christ World Missions exists around the world. Others who serve with MCC or parachurch organizations sent recipes. Several North American ethnic groups were also included. You enlarged our vision and broadened our horizons.

We acknowledge...
Geoff Isley's always available and expert assistance in layout and design.

We acknowledge...
Harriet Bicksler's faithful attendance at our committee meetings so she could capture the focus of our ideas.

We acknowledge...
Typesetter Heather Keefer who managed our work in addition to her busy family responsibilities.

We acknowlege...
The editing done by Martha Long, who provided her expertise so graciously.

We acknowledge...
Morris Sider's encouragement and invaluable guidance as the book progressed.

We acknowledge...
many others who gave generously of their time in collecting material, selecting scripture verses, typing, editing, or testing recipes, including: Ethel Bundy, JoAnne Brubaker, Karen Redfearn, Mildred Yoder, Marlene Comfort, Jennie Rensberry, Patti Miller, Judy Smith, Rita Steffee, Virginia Whittington, Anna Ruth Ressler, Anna Verle Miller, Shelly Engle, Dot Fries, Vivian Galebach, JoLene Hawbaker, Cathy Long, Tracy Thomas, Cathy Cline, Frank and Lois Kipe, Cindy Chisholm and various Sunday school and Bible study groups. It's true, without you this book would not have come into existence.

We also acknowledge...
Our friends and families who endured our cookbook conversations for years.

And finally, as editor, I acknowledge...
the committee members. How very much I have appreciated your capable assistance, A. J., Eleanor, Erma (Hoover), Ethel, Kas, Nancy and Ruth! You have made yourselves readily and faithfully available from the beginning to the end of the project. Your enthusiasm has made this an exciting experience for me. Beyond that, our friendships have deepened as we worked together. Thank you!

Our World of Hospitality

This map shows the locations where hospitality described in this book takes place.

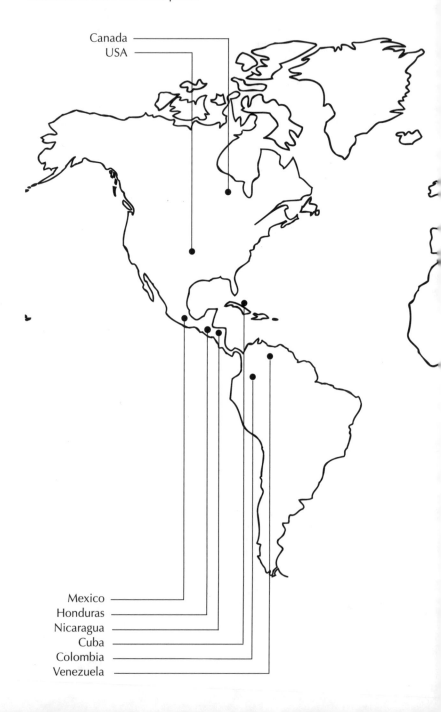

England ——————
Spain ——————

Canada ——————
USA ——————

Mexico ——————
Honduras ——————
Nicaragua ——————
Cuba ——————
Colombia ——————
Venezuela ——————

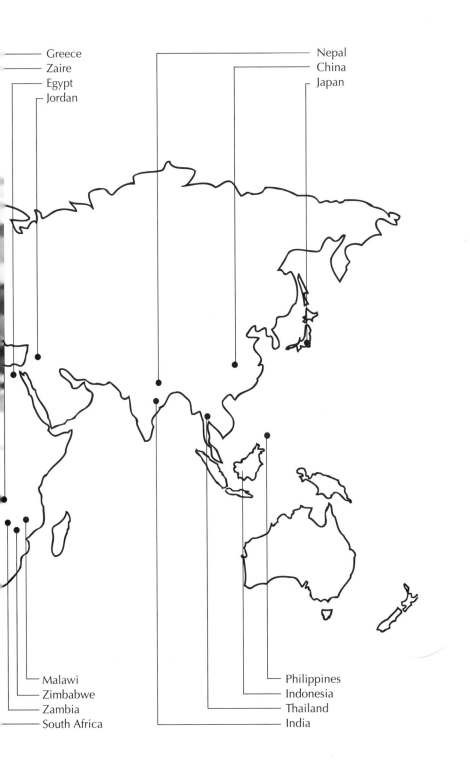

Greece
Zaire
Egypt
Jordan

Nepal
China
Japan

Malawi
Zimbabwe
Zambia
South Africa

Philippines
Indonesia
Thailand
India

Celebration of Hospitality

CONTENTS

A Celebration
of Hospitality

*I*MAGINE THE ARRIVAL 100 YEARS AGO OF THE FIRST
Brethren in Christ missionary party at what is now
Matopo Mission in Zimbabwe. Tired from months of
travel and decisions about where they would begin their
work, uncertain about what awaited them, yet exhilarated at
finally having arrived where they believed God had called them, they
met the people of Matabeleland. Depleted by a long war, the Ndebele
people were surprised by and perhaps a little suspicious of these white
folks, and curious about why they had come so far. Yet they were compelled by their own traditions of hospitality to welcome the strangers to
their midst. Before long, the Ndebeles treated their American guests to
a meal of stiff cornmeal porridge served with a relish made from wild
greens and accompanied by amahewu (a beverage made from
cornmeal). The Americans soon learned how to eat the stiff porridge
with their fingers, taking a small ball and dipping it into the relish for
each bite.

That's obviously not exactly how it happened, but it's how the 100-
year Brethren in Christ experience with international food, culture and
customs could have begun. One hundred years ago, when Jesse and
Elizabeth Engle, Frances Davidson and Alice Heise went to Africa, many
people's knowledge about cultures besides their own was relatively lim-
ited. Now, thanks to the technology of air travel, phones, fax machines,
satellite television, e-mail and internet connections, we have almost
instant access to places and people once thought exotic, unlearned and
unreachable, and we can make more accurate assessments about other
parts of the world.

The world has indeed become smaller in the sense that we can
easily and quickly communicate with almost any corner of the globe.

In addition, people are migrating in greater numbers than ever before. There are 125 million people who now live some place other than where they were born or hold their citizenship—an increase of 25 percent in the 1990s. Two percent of the world's people are legal or illegal immigrants, refugees, asylum seekers or migrant workers.

Despite these large numbers of people who have helped to mix the cultures and ethnicities of various countries around the world, the vast majority of people—98 percent—stay home and never move beyond the boundaries of their own countries. Of these, many have significant exposure to other cultures because people have moved to their countries and communities, but in some parts of the world, there is relatively little knowledge of or exposure to other peoples, cultures and customs. Even where there is the opportunity, other priorities can keep us ignorant. The world is still a big place.

On the one hand, then, this cookbook recognizes that as the result of increasing global interconnectedness and migration patterns, people all over the world can easily find out how and what others eat, and in many cases they can also buy, prepare and eat food native to other cultures. On the other hand, the book helps to break through some of the isolation that still prevents many from experiencing the rich diversity in the world.

Another international cookbook, published more than 40 years ago, observed that "the willingness to eat what others eat is one of the surest ways to learn something about the rest of the world" (Myra Waldo, *The Complete Round-the-World Cookbook*, New York: Doubleday and Co., 1954). This new cookbook, celebrating 100 years of Brethren in Christ World Missions, reiterates that truth.

A Celebration of Hospitality suggests that food is more than basic nutrition and physical sustenance, important as those are. Besides meeting nutritional needs and satisfying hunger, food helps connect us to others nearby and far away. It is an integral part of communal activities, and it is often an expression of not only our desire to be in relationship and to express our individuality.

Another way of saying much the same thing is to associate food customs with what psychologist Abraham Maslow calls a "hierarchy of human needs." At the most basic level, food meets the human need for survival. We eat to live. Food also provides safety and security, especially when families and societies are able to preserve and store food for the next year or perhaps the next decade so that when the next drought or pestilence strikes, there will be food to eat. Food is used to satisfy the human need for belongingness—eating together forges loving relationships. Food also contributes to self-esteem as people take pride in their preparing and serving food in attractive ways. The highest need, for self-actualization, is met through creative and innovative uses and preparation of food. (Paul Fieldhouse, Food and Nutrition: Customs and Culture. London, Croom Helm, 1986, pp. 25-29).

On the surface, it might seem as though poorer societies are stuck at the lower levels of survival and security, while the rich can indulge themselves in ways that contribute to their needs for self-esteem and self-actualization. The reality is, however, that some of the most creative and "self-actualizing" work with foods can happen in societies where the diet is basic by necessity and where there is not easy access to processed or prepared foods.

That creativity is reflected in this cookbook along with a vivid demonstration that the ability to extend hospitality does not depend on whether one is rich or poor. Extending hospitality is, however, often made more challenging by the lack of resources. That's why it is also good to remind ourselves that while we are celebrating food and hospitality, 35,000 people die every day for hunger-related reasons. According to Food for the Hungry, 300 million people are chronically hungry in Asia, 140 million in Africa, and 50 million live in absolute poverty in Latin America. Some of these people are undoubtedly our Brethren in Christ brothers and sisters.

Yet because we have experienced hospitality in many parts of the world, we know exactly what the apostle Paul was talking about when he described the generosity of the Macedonians: "Out of the most severe trial, their overflowing joy and their extreme poverty welled up in rich generosity … They gave as much as they were able, and even beyond their ability" (2 Cor. 8:2-3). It's the same thing Frances Davidson experienced from the Ndebele people in those early days of Brethren in Christ missions: "The people are always generous, and...food...is always shared with the strangers. No one needs to go through the country hungry unless there is famine, and even then they will often divide the last morsel" (*South and South Central Africa*, p. 205). So although those of us who have all the food we need should consider how we can share with people who don't have enough to eat, we can also learn much about hospitality from people in more difficult circumstances.

The ideas of celebration, hospitality and food that this book revolves around are firmly rooted in Scripture. Repeatedly in the Old Testament the people of Israel were instructed to "celebrate the festival" to com-memorate the end of their oppression in Egypt or some other significant event. Abraham entertained visitors who brought him unbelievable news; the family of Rebekah provided lodging and food for the party that had come to find Isaac a wife; Boaz allowed Naomi and Ruth to glean food from his fields; Elijah enjoyed the hospitality of the widow of Zarephath. And the list could go on.

Jesus' ministry often revolved around food—feeding the four and five thousand, having dinner at the home of Mary and Martha and Lazarus, attending the wedding in Cana, telling stories about wedding banquets and feasts, allowing the disciples to pick grain on the Sabbath because they were hungry, inviting himself "for tea" at the home of Zacchaeus, risking criticism by having dinner with sinners, celebrating a last supper with his disciples, eating breakfast with the eleven before he ascended to heaven. Paul relied on the hospitality of people like Lydia, the Philippian jailer, and Priscilla and Aquila in the towns and villages on his missionary route. When he was shipwrecked on the island of Malta, the "islanders showed unusual kindness" (Acts 28:2). The apostles' letters to churches exhorted believers to practice hospitality; in fact, potential church leaders were required to demonstrate hospitality.

The variety of celebrations and food events recorded in the Bible reinforce the centrality of food in our lives. Yes, we eat to live, but as has already been noted, eating is also important as a means of social interaction and communication. Food is a gift from God. Hospitality is also a gift, not only to accept graciously but to offer to others as well. When we share our food and our hospitality with others, we share a bit of ourselves. It is immaterial whether the meal is a one-pot dish cooked over an open fire with water and wood carried for miles, or an elegant seven-course catered dinner cooked in a technologically state-of-the-art kitchen with ingredients bought in a gourmet food store. What are important are the relationships forged, the conversations shared, and the part of ourselves that we give to someone else as we eat together.

The makings of simple meals and elaborate dinners plus other good things to eat and drink are in this cookbook. Use the book to find out about the food, customs and traditions of people you may not know well; try new recipes and foods even if they sound a little strange; experiment with uncommon ingredients; invite friends, neighbors and strangers to share your food and your hospitality. Celebrate!

A Celebration of Hospitality is more than a cookbook. It does indeed contain the requisite recipes to qualify it as a cookbook. But it is more importantly a celebration of the many saints "from every tribe and language and people and nation" who will gather in heaven because the Brethren in Christ for 100 years have extended God's offer of hospitality to the world.

APPETIZERS, BREADS, SNACKS AND BEVERAGES

"you have saved
the best till now"

—John 2:10

J esus' first miracle at the wedding in Cana, besides turning water into wine, also suddenly turned the bridegroom into a much more appealing host. The usual custom was to serve the best wine first and then bring out the cheaper wine after the guests had too much to drink. But when Jesus turned the water into wine, saving the bridegroom from social embarrassment, everyone thought the bridegroom had improved the custom and raised the standards for hospitality. His generosity apparently became the talk of the wedding feast because it went beyond expectations and custom.

Most cultures have expectations—some written and some simply understood—for hospitality by both hosts and guests. In Japan, for example, guests are expected to take a gift with them when they visit someone. This is such a significant part of the culture that entire industries have been created to cater to the needs of people who want to buy gifts to take when they visit friends and relatives. Protocols for gift-giving have prevailed for centuries. Sections of stores are devoted to pre-wrapped gifts (in pastel colors, not white or red) so one can quickly and easily run in a pick up a gift.

Hospitality also must be reciprocated. Guests at a Japanese wedding are expected to give money to the bride and groom, but they will receive several gifts from the bride and groom in return. These gifts need to be planned for when wedding arrangements are made, just as one would arrange for the reception, photography, flowers, etc. To make it easier, numerous catalogues are available from which to choose the right gifts.

The rituals associated with the tradition of hospitality gifts in Japan might seem to some like a burdensome way to fulfill one's social obligations, but they are one means by which a polite society expresses graciousness and generosity. The proper gift reflects one's inner feelings and knowledge of the personal interests of others. A gift graciously offered, however it is customarily done in specific cultures and at whatever point in the meeting the gift is given, is like the cold drink or snack one offers guests when they visit. Consider how you can offer as well as reciprocate the gift of hospitality as you try the appetizers, snacks, breads and beverages from around the world.

Spiced Tea
Nepal

Chiah
(chee-ah)

Serves 10

Wonderful on a cold, chilly and damp day to escape the gloom!

Bring to a full boil:
   10 c. water
Add:
   5 tea bags or 5 t. loose tea
   2 c. milk, heated
   8 whole cloves
   1 t. ground cardamom
   2 cinnamon sticks
Steep 5 to 10 minutes. Serve hot.

— *Esther Lenhert, Kathmandu, Nepal*

Fruit Drink
Venezuela

Batidos
(bah-TEE-dohs)

These drinks are served in restaurants, streetside coffee shops and at home. They are very refreshing on a hot day.

Combine in a blender:
   1-1$^1/_2$ c. fresh fruit
   $^1/_2$ c. water
   2-4 T. sugar, as desired
   5-6 ice cubes--add one at a time
Serve immediately.

Options:
Use chunks of frozen fruit and omit ice cubes.
Use milk instead of water.
Use any fruit or combination of fruit:
   Watermelon, strawberries, cantaloupe, papaya,
   pineapple, mango.
For an exotic and exquisite flavor, try orange
passion fruit and granadine syrup.

–*Martha Giles, Niagara Falls, ON (Caracas, Venezuela)*

Cold rice and cold tea are bearable but cold looks and cold words are not.

– *Japanese Proverb*

Yogurt Freshener
Nepal

Lassi
(LAH-see)

Mix all ingredients:
**1 qt. milk
1 qt. yogurt
$^1/_2$-$^3/_4$ c. sugar
4 t. vanilla
6-8 dry mint leaves**
Let stand in refrigerator at least 5 hours.

– Esther Lenhert, Kathmandu, Nepal

Pumpkin Punch
Colombia

Jugo de Auyama
(WHO-go
day Ow-YAH-mah)

Serves 8

Combine in blender:
**2 c. pumpkin, cooked
3 oz. package strawberry jello
2 or more cups milk
Add sugar as desired.**
Serve very cold.

Options: Other flavors of jello can be used and cranberry is especially satisfying.
Good for any occasion.

– Gloria Hernández de Silva, Niza 9, Bogota, Colombia

Just as in Jesus' time, in Zambia collecting water is a time of socializing. The women from the villages near a well or river go early in the morning for water. In drought conditions they go to the well at 4 a.m. before the water level drops and they are unable to collect water. The women spend the time waiting in line to socialize with the other women before they go home to begin their day's work.

– Ann Marie Parry, Danville, PA (Choma, Zambia)

Root Beer
Pennsylvania Dutch

1 Gallon

Dissolve:
>   1 t. dry yeast in ¹/₂ c. warm water
>   2 c. sugar in 1 qt. hot water

Combine above in a gallon jar. Add:
>   **4 T. root beer extract**
>   **Warm water to fill jar**

Stir until all ingredients are well combined.
Cover jar.
Set in warm sun for 4 hours.
The root beer will be ready to drink the next day.
Chill before serving.

– Arlene Martin, Elizabethtown, PA

Lemon Barley Water
England

Wash **2 T. pearl barley**. Put in a large pan with **4 cups water** and bring to a boil.
Grate and add to the water:
>   **2 lemons, rind only**

Cover and leave to cool.
Squeeze the lemons and add the juice to the above mixture.
Strain the mixture through a sieve. Sweeten to taste.

– Judy Smith, London, England

Tea Scones
Zimbabwe

Makes 16

When the missionaries spent a day shopping in Bulawayo, Zimbabwe, the tradition was to meet at Haddon and Sly Tea Lounge about mid-morning for tea and toasted scones. Other foods were available but scones were bought more often than anything else.

Measure into bowl:
2 c. flour
3 T. sugar
3 t. baking powder
¹/₄ t. salt
Add and chop with pastry blender:
¹/₃ c. margarine
Combine and pour into above:
1 egg, beaten
¹/₂ c. milk
Stir quickly and lightly until no flour shows. Add more milk if needed to make a soft dough. Turn the dough out on a floured surface and knead gently about one minute. Roll out about one-half inch thick; cut into 2-inch rounds. Place on ungreased baking sheet; bake at 425° for 12 minutes. Serve warm.

– Erma Hoover, Mechanicsburg, PA
(Zimbabwe)

Half-way to the mountain village of Lamao in the Philippines is Subusub. Tinguian hospitality assures us that a rest stop with a good meal awaits us. The stop will last at least two hours–the fire must be stirred, a chicken killed, dressed and cooked, and the rice cooked.

The people of Subusub care for us as they do for their own. And, during the rainy season, they may advise us to stay over for the night. Then we can go on, refreshed, in the morning.

– J. Wilmer Heisey,
Mount Joy, PA

English
Scones
Canada

12 scones

Stir together in a large bowl:
  2¹/₄ c. flour
  2 T. granulated sugar
  2¹/₂ t. baking powder
  ¹/₂ t. baking soda
  ¹/₂ t. salt
Using a pastry blender, cut in until mixture resembles coarse crumbs:
  ¹/₂ c. cold butter, cubed
Stir in:
  ¹/₂ c. currants
Add all at once, stirring with fork to make soft, sticky dough:
  1 c. buttermilk
With lightly-floured hands press dough into a ball. On lightly-floured surface, knead gently 10 times. Pat dough into ³/₄-inch high round. Cut into 2¹/₂-inch rounds. Place on ungreased baking sheet. Bake at 425° for 12-15 minutes.

Options:
A tea-time treat. Serve with jam and/or whipped, unsweetened cream.

– Laureen Ginder, Elizabethtown, PA

Lord Jesus, I'm sorry. Sometimes I think about food too much. I dream of all the delicious things there are to eat when I really should be doing other things. Please help me not to make food so important, and help me not to be greedy at mealtimes. Amen.

*– 365 Children's prayers, written and compiled by Carol Watson.
1989, Lion Publishing P.C., Sandy Lane West,
Little more, Oxford, England*

Everyone Is a Relative

My husband Jethro was born and grew up in the country. I had the best of both worlds because I was born in the city but spent all my school holidays in the country on Grandfather's farm. In recent years, as we have observed our children growing up in the city, we have felt that they were missing out on a very important aspect of our culture. We therefore looked around and set up home in a village amidst the hills of Matopo.

It is now almost four years since we moved, but we have never ceased to be amazed by the welcoming and loving spirit of the rural folk who are our neighbors. As soon as we get out to the village a neighbor will send over a basket of nuts, a few ears of corn, a pumpkin or some sweet potatoes and say, "Naka Bongani"(Mother of Bongani) or "MaMoyo" (Moyo is my maiden name and sometimes I am called by it), here is a little something for my children/grandchildren."

You see, in the country everyone is everyone's relative. Another time someone will say, "Here are some mangoes. I was afraid we'd eat up all the fruit before you came and my grandchildren would miss out. Here, take these, I have been saving them for you."

I'd send back the basket with a loaf of bread, a packet of tea or a few potatoes. (Culturally, it helps to build relationships and strengthen bridges if the container is not sent back empty.)

During another visit I try to get ahead of my neighbors and send out a bar of soap or a second-hand sweater to a needy person. Sometimes I will go and ask for a few matches in order to start a fire. This is a way of saying "We need and depend on each other." It makes it easier for a neighbor to say, "Today there is no food for the family. May I have a bucket-full of mealie-meal?" or "I have a headache. Do you have a pain killer?"

Such love is overwhelming. I used to protest but now I have learned to accept graciously whatever comes. Rural life is such that no family can fail to plough the land because they have no plough or cattle or no one should walk about naked. Community life demands that people should care for each other regardless of social status.

– Doris Dube, Bulawayo, Zimbabwe

Fastnachts
Pennsylvania Dutch

Fastnacht
(Fahst-NAHKT)

Makes 4 dozen

*We gather as a family for this occasion: Sons, daughter, daughters-in-law, son-in-law, and grandchildren. Sometime before Fastnacht Day we all come to our home and enjoy the day making Fastnachts.
We double the recipe several times so each family has some to take home. This recipe is over 100 years old.*

Dissolve in ¼ c. warm water:
  2 oz. cake yeast
Add and mix:
  4 c. warm water
  1 c. sugar
  ⅔ c. shortening, melted
  2 T. salt
Add gradually and knead:
  3½ lb. flour
Place dough in a bowl, cover with cloth and allow to rise 1 hour.
Remove dough from bowl and roll out ½-inch thick (use desired size biscuit cutter) and cut fastnachts.
Let rise again for 1 hour. Then fry in deep fat until each side is lightly browned.

Fastnacht Day is the day before Lent begins. The custom began as a way to use up all the fat before the beginning of Lent.

– Janie Hess, Conestoga, PA

Editor's note: Christians of Germanic origin held a festival on the last day before Lent, a day of merrymaking before the Lenten fasting. Fastnachts were traditionally eaten on this day which was also called Shrove Tuesday and Pancake Day.

My Favorite Bread
Québec

Mon Pain Preferé
(Mohn pain
preh-fair-ay)

4 loaves

Dissolve 2 T. (or 2 packages) **dry yeast** in $^1/_2$ c. **warm water**
Add to above and set aside:
  1 t. sugar
  $^1/_4$ t. ginger
Mix together in a large bowl:
  $^1/_3$ c. sugar
  $^3/_4$ c. dry milk powder
  2$^1/_2$ c. warm water
  4 c. flour (all purpose or 2 c. whole
  wheat, 2 c. white)
Add yeast mixture.
Mix to a smooth batter; beat well. Allow to rise until light and bubbly (about 15 minutes)
Stir down and add:
  3 c. warm water
  5 t. salt
  $^1/_2$ c. shortening or lard
  8 c. white bread flour (approximately)
Knead 5 minutes, using additional flour if necessary. Place in greased bowl, turn, let rise until double (approximately 1 hour).
Punch down. Divide dough in 4 parts and shape into loaves. Place in greased 9x5-inch bread pans. Cover and let rise 45 minutes. Bake at 350° for 25 minutes and at 325° for 20 minutes.

– Sylvie St-Hilaire, St. Romuald, Québec

He who has an ear, let him hear what the Spirit says to the churches. To him who overcomes, I will give the right to eat from the tree of life, which is in the paradise of God.

– Revelation 2:7

Fry Bread
New Mexico

Navajo

Serves about 12

Mix together in a large mixing bowl:
- 4 c. flour
- 1 T. baking powder
- 1 t. salt
- 2 T. powdered milk

Add gradually, mixing with a fork:
- 1½ c. **warm water (more or less)**

Make a soft dough. Cover. Let rest 10-20 minutes.

In an electric fry pan, heat to 400-425°:
- **1 inch oil**

Divide dough into 12 pieces. Flatten and pull a piece of dough into a flat round (about 6 inches in diameter). Fry in hot oil, turning once until brown on both sides, about 1½ minutes on each side. Serve at once.

Tortilla variation:
To the above dry ingredients add:
- **3 T. shortening**

Cook in a dry pan about 20 seconds on each side.

Another variation: Serves 9
- **3 c. flour**
- **2½ t. baking powder**
- **2 t. salt**
- **2 T. powdered milk**
- **1 c. + 1 T. water**

Dough can be made 6 hours ahead and fried when ready to eat. Also good used as shells for tacos.

– *Millie Imboden, Mechanicsburg, PA*

Festive Ham Bread
Venezuela

Pan de Jamón
(Pahn day hah-MOHN)

This is a favorite Venezuelan Christmas treat. It is also served at many special church functions.

Make your favorite white bread recipe for 2 loaves. Let rise, punch down and divide into 2 halves. (Or defrost 2 loaves of frozen bread dough.)

Roll each into a rectangle approximately ¹/₄ inch thick. Spread lightly with bacon grease, margarine or mustard, if desired.
Layer on each rectangle:
  ¹/₄ lb. cooked ham, sliced or diced
  ¹/₃ c. bacon, fried and crumbled
  ¹/₃ - ¹/₂ c. stuffed olives, sliced
  ¹/₃ - ¹/₂ c. raisins
Roll up dough as for jelly roll, turning ends under, and place on greased cookie sheet, seam side down. Do not let rise, but bake immediately at 350° for 30-35 minutes.
Vary the amounts and kinds of ingredients according to taste.

To serve: When bread has cooled slightly, cut into 1-inch slices. It can be sliced thinner or thicker, depending upon the number of people to serve. Serve hot or cold.

– Martha Giles, Niagara
Falls, ON and
Sherry Holland, Caracas,
Venezuela

Making bannock

18

Kneeldown Bread
Navajo

This bread gets its name from kneeling down in order to grind the corn.

Scrape the kernels of corn from **fresh corn on the cob**. Grind it on a metate, a flat stone, or use a food processor to finely chop the corn. Don't completely grind it to a smooth paste as it should still be slightly chunky. Shape this corn into small loaves of bread about 1 1/2 inches by 4 inches in size. Wrap them in several layers of fresh green corn husks. They can either be baked in hot ashes for 1 hour or baked in the oven at medium low temperature for at least one hour. Remove from husks and eat at once.

– Karen Redfearn, New Mexico

Fresh Corn Bread
Zimbabwe

Serves 6

My mother used to bake fresh corn bread in a three-legged pot. She would put sand in the pot and put charcoal on the lid and under the pot. When the pot was hot, she would put the mixture in a metal bowl and bake it inside the black pot. This was a delicacy for her children who returned home for school vacation from mission centers at Matapo, Wanezi, and Mtshabezi.

2 c. corn, fresh or frozen
1 t. salt
1/2 c. flour
1 t. sugar
1 1/2 t. baking powder
3 T. oil
1/2 c. milk

Combine all ingredients and mix thoroughly.
Pour into a greased baking dish.
Bake at 350° for 45-60 minutes or until golden brown.

May be served with a meal or with syrup for tea.

– Martha Sibanda, Diana's Pool, Zimbabwe

Bannock
Northern
Canada:
Cree and Dene

Serves 8-10

Mix together like biscuit dough:
$2^1/2$ c. flour
2 t. baking powder
1 t. salt
$^1/2$ c. lard
Add approximately 1 c. water
Stir until dough clings together, then knead on floured surface. Pat dough to one inch thickness and prick with a fork.
Bake on cookie sheet at 350°– 375° until well done.

The Native People do not usually store their bannock in any kind of wrap. They make three to four at a time, then stack them sideways on the table or counter against the wall. Lard, margarine or jam is spread on the bannock. The bannock dough can be wrapped around the end of a stick (grease stick) and baked over hot low coals. It is traditional to sit around the campfire at the end of the day, bake bannock on a stick, tell stories and drink tea.

– Jennie Rensberry, La Loche, Saskatchewan
– Marlene Comfort, La Ronge, Saskatchewan
– Greg Charles, Saskatchewan, Canada

Dear friend, you are faithful in what you are doing for the brothers, even though they are strangers to you. They have told the church about your love. You will do well to send them on their way in a manner worthy of God. ... We ought therefore to show hospitality to such men so that we may work together for the truth.

– 3 John 5, 6, 8

Blueberry Muffins
Cree

Makes 12 muffins

Combine:
  2 c. all purpose flour, sifted
  3 t. baking powder
  3 t. sugar
  ¹/₄ t. salt
  ³/₄ t. cinnamon
Combine and add to dry ingredients, stirring only enough to moisten:
  ³/₄ c. milk
  1 egg
  ¹/₂ c. butter, melted
Fold in:
  1 c. blueberries
Fill each muffin tin ²/₃ full. Bake for 25 minutes at 400°.

These are popular in the fall when blueberries are fresh. They are found at our church potluck suppers or sold at a food table for a fundraiser event.

– Ricky Sanderson, Saskatchewan, Canada

Cornbread Dressing
Southern United States

Serves 12

Sauté:
  1 c. celery, chopped
  ¹/₄ c. onions, chopped
  ³/₄ c. butter or margarine
Combine in large bowl:
  celery mixture
  5 c. biscuits, crumbled, or
      dry bread cubes
  5 c. cornbread, crumbled
  1 t. poultry seasoning
  ¹/₂ t. pepper
  4 c. or 2 - 14¹/₂ oz. cans chicken broth
Blend well.
Put mixture in a greased 9x13-inch pan and bake at 350° for 1 hour or until lightly browned.
Serve with chicken or turkey.

– Jodie Martin, Smithville, TN

Egg-Lemon Soup
Greece

Serves 6-8

Greek families did not all eat at the same time. Because of schedules, soups were prepared in the morning before the wife went to the field. When a family member came home the soopa was heated.

I serve the soopa with crusty bread and a light dessert when entertaining.

Prepare 7-8 c. soup stock by boiling **1 whole chicken or 2 chicken breasts** in sufficient water. Salt to taste.
Add:
¹/₂ -1 c. uncooked rice
cooked chicken, deboned
Mix in small bowl with a small amount of cooled stock:
1 T. cornstarch
2 eggs, beaten
Slowly stir into the rice and chicken mixture. Be careful it does not become stringy. Remove from heat.
Add:
1 T. butter or margarine
Slowly stir in:
juice of ¹/₂ lemon
Season with:
salt and pepper, to taste.
If desired, when serving top with:
1 t. parsley, chopped

– Beulah Heisey, Mechanicsburg, PA (Greece)

Egg and Lemon Soup
England

Serves 4

Put in a saucepan and bring to a boil:
6 c. chicken stock
Add and simmer for 15 minutes or until tender:
1 c. rice
Mix:
4 eggs, well beaten
juice of 2 lemons
Stir in a few spoonfuls of stock. Stir this mixture into the remaining stock. Cook gently for 3 minutes. Season to taste with salt and pepper.

– June Simmonds, London, England

Peanut Soup
Zambia

Serves 6

often serve this to overseas visitors. When ack and Trudy McClane visited, I served this soup or lunch. They enjoyed it o much that they nsisted I submit it for nclusion in this cookbook.

Soak overnight:
  2 c. raw peanuts
Drain off water. Add $1/2$ t. vegetable oil to nuts and water to cover. Cook $1^1/2$ hours or pressure cook 20 minutes.
Sauté and set aside:
  3 lg. tomatoes, cut in wedges
  1 green pepper, diced
  $1/2$ of 1 lg. onion, diced
Brown:
  $3/4$ lb. hamburger
  remainder of onion, diced
  Combine peanuts, tomato mixture, and meat.
Add and simmer 20-30 minutes:
  $1^1/2$ c. water
  2 c. tomato juice
  2 cubes beef bouillon
  $1^1/2$ t. chili powder
  $1/2$ t. chili seasoning mix (optional)
  $1/4$ t. garlic powder
  2 T. ketchup
  $1^1/2$ t. salt
  oregano
  3 T. sugar

The secret of this soup is to taste and retaste as you add seasonings until you reach the desired flavor. The amount of seasonings can be altered to suit individual tastes. Serve any time when soup is appropriate. It goes nicely with bran muffins and also with rice or stiff cornmeal porridge (nshima).

– *Phyllis A. Engle, Livingstone, Zambia*

What is Sweeter than Honey?

Upon our returning to the Philippines after twenty one years, my former students entertained me in the same house they had turned over to me in 1947. After Tomas, the first tenor, arrived from Sallapadan, the male quartet started singing. Federico presented me with a large bottle of wild honey. What could I do with it, at the beginning of a long journey that would take me to India, Kenya, Zambia, Zimbabwe, Nigeria, and England? But then Jose brought in some green banana leaves to wrap the honey bottle for travel and twisted some wild vine to tie the case and provide a handle so it could be carried on a stick on the trail to the lowland. That bottle, twenty five years later, rests on the mantle in our family room today.

Ten years later, with my wife Velma by my side, I made another trip to Lamao, this time by jeep all the way, on what they called a road! The women came and picked up Velma, with every evidence of love and affection. We heard them sing again!

Returning through Subusub, we were met by Pedro Batoon, now the high school principal there. To Velma, with whom he used to banter about the relative merits of milk and tobacco, Pedro said, "Mom, I no longer smoke," and he handed her a large bottle of wild honey. That square bottle of exquisite sweetness had to go with us. We shared some of it with Harvey Sider at a leaders' training conference in Madhipura, Bihar, India. Today it, too, rests on the mantle in our family room.

David said:
The fear of the Lord
is clean, enduring forever; the judgments of the Lord
are true and righteous altogether.
More to be desired are they than gold,
Yea, than much fine gold: Sweeter also than honey and
the honeycomb.
Moreover by them is thy servant warned:
And in keeping of them there is great reward.
Psalm 19:9-11(KJV)

– J. Wilmer Heisey, Mount Joy, PA

Pumpkin Soup
Venezuela

Crema de Auyama
(Cre-ma day ow-YAH-mah)

Serves 4-6

Heat 1 T. margarine or oil in large sauce pan.
Add and sauté:
> 2 cloves garlic, chopped

Add and bring to boil:
> 2 c. chicken broth

Add:
> 5 c. fresh pumpkin, pared and cut into one-inch cubes.

Cook until transparent.
Puree in blender.

This is a favorite soup of the people of Venezuela.

– Sherry Holland, Caracas, Venezuela

It's a special market day in village Malawi. School children and adults, too, are lined up along the road waiting their turn to buy mkati (hm-ker-tey). If we look over their shoulders we can see the vendors busy cutting washed banana leaves into squares. Then they mash ripe bananas and mix them well with sugar and corn meal. Now comes the tricky part. The mkati makers dip their hands in cold water, then fold the sticky mixture into the banana leaves, being careful that the leaf-folding makes a square shape. Into a pot of boiling water they go, bubble 20 minutes or so and out comes the sweet and satisfying mkati, perfect to eat with a cup of tea or a cold drink.

– Based on a recipe from Helegima Chimkango, Kuphanga Village, Malawi

Lemon Grass Soup
Thailand

Serves 4-6

Boil over medium heat:
   3 c. water
Add and cook until meat is soft:
   1 root lemon grass, chopped in thin rings
   1-2 chili peppers, chopped
   1/2 yellow onion, chopped
   Meat – any kind you like: shrimp, chicken, fish, and even tofu if you are a vegetarian
Add and simmer:
   1-2 large red tomatoes, chopped
   2 t. fish sauce
   2 T. lemon or lime juice
   1/3 can straw mushrooms
   3-4 slices of ginger (Thai ginger is best)
Add before turning off the stove:
   2 T. green onions, chopped
   2 Kafir lime leaves
   2 T. Chinese parsley, chopped
Taste and enjoy!

– Kathy Brubaker, Grantham, PA
(Bangkok, Thailand)

I enjoyed trying out recipes from Thailand and found most of the ingredients at a Thai store in Harrisburg, Pennsylvania.

The lemon grass looked like miniature bamboo grass. To prepare lemon grass, strip off the outer leaves and finely chop the inside core into thin rings. Boil in water to extract the lemon flavor and then discard. They can be eaten but are very tough. The leaves can also be added when you steep black tea to give a lemon flavor. It makes great iced tea, also.

I found lemon grass plants being sold in our nursery. I planted it in my garden and it thrived. It was wonderful to have fresh lemon grass to use all summer. I recommend growing your own. It is tender, however, and needs to be potted and brought inside during our PA winters.

– Ruth Zook,
Mechanicsburg, PA

Mulligatawny Soup
India

Serves 4

Sauté until golden brown (keep from burning):
 3 T. oil
 2 medium onions, finely chopped
Add and simmer 20 minutes:
 2 bay leaves
 1 t. coriander
 ¼ t. turmeric
 ½ t. cumin
 6 pepper corns
 4 whole cloves
 2 small pieces stick cinnamon
 ½ t. salt
 ¼ t. red pepper
 1 T. curry powder
 3 c. chicken broth or water
Add and continue heating:
 2 cans cream of chicken soup
If desired add ½ c. cooked rice
Simmer for 15 minutes.
 Add **lemon juice** at serving time.

Good for a light supper served with Indian bread (chappatis) or pita bread (whole wheat).

– Kalim Mohmad, India

"Add more water to the broth." (We're coming to dinner!)

– Colombian saying

Roasted Peanuts
Zambia

Musuka
(Moo-soo-kah)

6 Servings

Roast at 350° for 20-25 minutes until slightly brown, stirring frequently:
> **2 c. raw peanuts**

Combine and pour over hot peanuts:
> **³/₄ t. salt**
> **1 c. water**

Continue roasting peanuts until moisture is absorbed. Serve as a snack or at the end of a meal as a dessert.

– Shelly Muleya, Mizinga Village, Choma, Zambia

Option:
For a special occasion, toss hot peanuts with seasoned salt.

Seasoned salt
Combine:
> **1 cup salt**
> **1 t. garlic powder**
> **1 t. onion powder**
> **1 T. paprika**
> **1 T. sugar**
> **1 t. turmeric**

Combine and place in a jar with a shaker top. Use as seasoned salt on vegetables, peanuts, popcorn, etc.

– Ann Marie Parry, Danville, PA (Choma,Zambia))

My students learned to know one of my favorite snacks—roasted ants. After a rainy day clouds of ants would ascend from the anthills. As they flew around a source of light the wings dropped off and the bodies fell to the floor. These the young people collected and roasted in a hot pot. The half-inch toasted body was soon ready to eat and a cupful offered to me. I ate them with delight and thought they tasted like bacon!

– Anna R. Wolgemuth,
Mechanicsburg, PA
(Zimbabwe)

Soft Pretzels
Pennsylvania/ Germany

Makes 12 pretzels

Because meat and dairy products were not eaten at Lent, people lived largely on breads and pastries. Bakers in Germany in the fifth century decided to turn out something that even looked religious. The crossed arms of the pretzel were intended to represent a Christian at prayer with palms on opposite shoulders making a criss-cross.

Pennsylvania is the "pretzel capital" of the United States. Our family enjoyed making these soft pretzels as a Friday "Family Night" activity when our six children were growing up.

Dissolve in 1^1/$_2$ c. water:
  2 packets of yeast
Add:
  ^{1}/$_2$ t. salt
  4 c. unsifted bread flour
Mix ingredients together, knead briefly and form into a ball. Cover with a damp cloth and allow to rest 15 minutes.
In a small bowl dissolve:
  ^{1}/$_4$ c. baking soda
  1 c. cool water.
(The soda will not totally dissolve, therefore needs to be stirred occasionally.)
Divide dough into 12 equal pieces and roll into 8-inch ropes.
Soak two at a time in baking soda water for 1-2 minutes. Pat lightly with paper towel and shape on greased baking sheet (5-6 per sheet).
Sprinkle with coarse salt as desired. Bake at 350° for 20 minutes.

Coarse salt can be found in health stores or specialty shops.

– Faithe Hoffman, Palmyra, PA

Is it not to share your food with the hungry and to provide the poor wanderer with shelter – when you see the naked, to clothe him, and not to turn away from your own flesh and blood?
– Isaiah 58:7

Salties
Nepal

Nimki
(NIM-kee)

Serves 12-15

Using a pastry blender, mix as for pastry:
2 c. whole wheat flour
2 T. cumin seed, ground
2 T. onion salt
¹/₂ t. salt
4 T. oil
Knead thoroughly until elastic.
Divide into 5-6 balls. Flour a pastry board and roll out dough. Cut in strips diagonally ³/₄-inch wide.
Deep fry until golden brown at a temperature of 350°. Lift from hot oil and dry on paper towels. Salt to taste. Cool and eat as a snack.

– Esther Lenhert, Kathmandu, Nepa

Landon Charles and I were on a ten-day trek into the remote interior of NE Abra Province in the Philippines, possibly the first Americans to have walked there since World War II. Entering a small barrio, we were invited to come up into the bamboo house, built on posts, three to four feet above the ground.

Soon we were offered two fine fat green worms, a bit larger and longer than our largest finger. With just a bit of hesitation, we accepted the gift treat, and our hosts began roasting them over an open fire. The roasted worms were not totally unlike a wiener.

– J. Wilmer Heisey,
Mount Joy, PA

I remember village visits for evangelism and visiting the sick when appreciation was expressed tangibly for our visit. The host or hostess "didn't want us to return empty-handed" so a snack was offered for the walk or ride back to the mission. The snack might be watermelon, cooked yams (now cold and refreshing), or peanuts which were steamed or boiled previously and dropped into our hands (the Spanish, red-skinned peanuts were the favorites). In those earlier days there was very little shortage of food. The host was able to give and usually had food left for the family.

– Anna Wolgemuth,
Mechanicsburg, PA
(Zimbabwe)

Vegetable Fritters
India

Pakoras
(pa-KOR-ahs)

Serves 6

Sift:
  1/2 c. besan (ground lentils) flour
  1/4 t. baking powder
Add:
  1/2 t. turmeric
  1 t. coriander powder
  1/2 t. red ground chili
  salt to taste
Gradually add water to make a batter.
To batter add:
  2 medium onions, chopped
Drop by teaspoonfuls into hot fat or oil and deep fry until crisp.
Potatoes, eggplant, cauliflower or spinach, cut in small pieces, may also be used. Dip into batter and deep fry.

– Kas Bert, Carlisle, PA

31

Tostones
Nicaragua

(Tohs-TOH-ness)

Peel 2-3 green plantains
These look like bananas but are longer and thicker. They can be green or starting to turn yellow-brown. They need to be peeled with a knife. Cut them into 3/4-1 inch slanted slices. One plantain will give 6-7 slices.
Fry in about 1/4-inch oil in frying pan over medium heat. Fry on both sides until they look yellow, not golden crispy brown. Remove from pan. Fold some wax paper in half. Place a slice of plantain inside the paper and smash the slice to about half its original height. The bottom of a wide glass works nicely to smash them.
Return the plantains to the pan and fry again until slightly golden on both sides. Remove from pan and drain on absorbent paper before serving. Sprinkle with salt if desired.

These are good served with any meal or as a snack.

– Maritza Mairena, Managua, Nicaragua

Chappatis are round, flat Indian bread made from whole wheat flour. To one cup of flour and one half teaspoon salt, add water gradually to moisten (similar to baking powder biscuit dough). Knead for five minutes until some-what elastic. Set aside for 30 minutes if you have time before the meal. Shape dough into six balls and roll out to a five-inch diameter with rolling pin on flat, floured surface.

Heat a non-stick frying pan until very hot and fry the chappatis on both sides, holding down gently around edges with a small clean cloth or a pancake turner until slightly brown. Then press carefully in center to puff the chappati. While the chappati is frying, a delightful aroma fills the house. Serve hot with a vegetable curry or as a bread with a simple soup.

Samosas
India

(sah-MOH-sahs)

Makes about 20
pastries

Pastry:
Sift into a bowl:
   1½ c. white flour
   1 t. baking powder
   ½ t. salt
Add:
   2 T. melted butter or salad oil
   4 T. yogurt
Knead into a pliable dough.

Filling:
Sauté in 2 T. butter for 2 minutes:
   1 small onion, chopped fine
Add and sauté for five minutes:
   1 lb. potatoes, boiled and cut fine
   2 green chilies, minced
Add and mix thoroughly:
   1 t. curry powder
   1 t. salt
Remove from heat and cool.
Knead pastry again. Take small walnut-size piece
of pastry and shape into round ball. Flatten and
roll out on a floured board. Make thin and round
the size of a saucer. Cut in half. Make into a cone,
seal with water, fill and press together. When all
the samosas are ready, fry in deep fat until crisp
and golden.

– A. J. Mann, Elizabethtown, PA (Bihar, India)

"Give bread to those who are hungry and hunger for You to
those who have bread."

– Prayer heard in Nicaraguan friend's home by Karen Poe

Her name is MaTshuma. She lived in a house right in the center of a cluster of match box houses typical of the vast majority of dwellings in that particular suburb. Her house was no different from that of her neighbors on either side of her. Even the color was the same. However, for some reason, unknown to her even now, beggars and travellers always seemed to end up at her door step. They'd ask for all sorts of things ranging from water to drink to requests like a blanket to shield one from the elements. MaTshuma never had the heart to turn a stranger away. For those asking for water, she'd also give a glass full of "amahewu." If food was asked for, she'd give "inkobe" or whatever the family was having that day. There was never much for the family but somehow MaTshuma learned to stretch it to share with a stranger. Both MaTshuma and her now grown children have been richly blessed by these encounters because they realize that this sharing is a way of ministering to fellow human beings.

"Amahewu" is a brew made out of corn meal mixed with ground millet which makes it ferment. The corn meal may be leftover thick porridge (sitshwala) from a meal. All this is mashed in water and left to ferment. It is usually served as a snack to quench thirst, especially for hard-working people on hot days.

"Inkobe" is a snack made up of peanuts, round nuts, beans and corn (maize) all cooked together.

– Doris Dube, Bulawayo, Zimbabwe

SALADS

"rejoice in all the
good things the
Lord your God
has given to you"
— Deut. 26:11

For awhile my congregation held monthly salad suppers for women as an opportunity for fellowship and outreach. Each woman brought a salad to share, and the serving table became a wonderful and colorful array of vegetables and fruits combined in many different ways. Like many other congregations, we also have potluck dinners periodically. Again these are often large, extravagant, delicious displays of food. At Thanksgiving, North Americans celebrate all the bounty that God has given us by gathering as extended families and friends over a meal that is much bigger than we really need.

More important than the food at these gatherings is the sense of community that they engender. In fact, "communal feasts" have a long history and are celebrated in all civilizations. They commemorate significant events, both religious and secular, honor people who have contributed to society, celebrate the harvest, promote knowledge and understanding of one's heritage, preserve cultural customs and traditions, and are acts of self-expression. The Chinese New Year is a month-long celebration in January and February. India commemorates the birthday of Mahatma Gandhi on October 2 each year with a festival called Gandhi Jayanti. The Kwanzaa festival, introduced into the United States from Africa, promotes family unity, cultural self-determination, responsibility, purpose, creativity and faith among African Americans.

Feasts and festivals can easily be criticized for their extravagance and waste, whether by wealthy people who are accused of being irresponsible with their resources or by poorer people who can ill afford to use what little they have on big once-and-done celebrations. Yet the human spirit needs times of celebration and extravagance.

Latin American festivals illustrate this truth. Amid much poverty and conflict, many Latin American countries celebrate with huge parades, music and revelry, lots of food and elaborate artistic displays, including intricate flower designs on the streets that can be trampled in an instant. What is the point, some might ask? Couldn't the money be put to better use? When we ask those questions, we are forgetting that festivals like these bring people together and remind them of their common humanity and their reliance on God even in the midst of extreme circumstances. In addition, sometimes these festivals function as a means of economic leveling as wealthy people spend large sums of money on food and drink, fireworks and decorations that everyone can enjoy.

The salad and condiment recipes that follow complement a basic diet. Salads are not usually the main food event and therefore could be considered unnecessary, perhaps even an extravagance. But not only can they serve the function of using up leftover foodstuffs, cleaning out the garden at the end of the season, or providing healthy nutrients our bodies need, they can also demonstrate the importance of times of communi⁺ celebrations.

Tamaulipeca Salad
Mexico

Ensalada Tamaulipeca
(En-sah-LAH-da tah-mow-lee-PAY-kah)

Serves 6

Mix together well:
   4-6 carrots, grated
   4 apples, peeled and cubed
   1-2 c. pineapple, drained and cubed
   1 c. mayonnaise
   ¹/₂ c. raisins
   pineapple juice as desired

This is an easy and nutritious dish and is typical of the Tamaulipas area.

– *Gracely Vázquez Espinosa,*
Ciudad Victoria, Tamps, Mexico

Greek Salad

In large bowl mix:
   1 small head lettuce,
      torn into bite-size pieces
   3 medium tomatoes, cut up
   ³/₄ c. black olives,
      pits removed and sliced in halves
   1 medium onion, sliced in rings
   ¹/₂ small head of cauliflour,
      cut into bite-size pieces
Mix:
   1 c. plain nonfat yogurt
   1 T. olive oil
   2 T. lemon juice
   1 t. oregano
   1¹/₂ t. dry mustard
   ¹/₂ t. salt
   ¹/₄ t. black pepper
Toss with vegetables. Sprinkle with pepper. Chill.

– *Beulah Heisey,*
Mechanicsburg, PA (MCC Greece)

Editor's Note: When our cookbook committee met, we used the opportunity to test and taste recipes we had received. The group enjoyed this salad served with moussaka.

Salada la Valenciana
Spain

Serves 6

Combine in salad bowl and toss thoroughly:
  1 thick slice French bread,
      rubbed with **1 large garlic clove** and
      broken into pieces
  Romaine lettuce,
      broken into bite-size pieces
  3 large oranges, peeled and sectioned
  4-oz. can pimentos, cut in strips
  1 medium onion, thinly sliced
  10-12 pimento-stuffed olives
  $^1/_4$ c. olive oil
Add and toss again:
  salt and pepper
  2 T. red wine vinegar

– Merly Bundy, Madrid, Spain

Cabbage Slaw For Freezer
Pennsylvania Dutch

Mix and let stand for 1 hour:
  1 medium head cabbage, shredded
  1 t. salt
Combine for dressing:
  1 c. vinegar
  $^1/_4$ c. water
  2 c. sugar
  1 t. mustard seed
  1 t. celery seed
Boil 1 minute then cool.
At the end of the hour squeeze excess moisture
out of the cabbage.
Add:
  1 green pepper, chopped
  1 carrot, grated
  1 c. celery, chopped
Then add cooled dressing and mix well.
Put in containers and freeze. It can be refrozen.

– Anna Ruth Ressler, Elizabethtown, PA

Cabbage Relish
Pennsylvania Dutch

Makes 5-6 pints

Grind the vegetables fine with hand grinder, or food processor using the 1-star blade:
  1 large cabbage
  4 green peppers
  5 medium carrots
  6 onions
Mix with ¹/₄ c. salt and let stand for 2 hours. Drain well.
Add:
  3 c. sugar
  1¹/₂ pt. cider vinegar
  ¹/₂ T. celery seed
  ¹/₂ T. mustard seed
Mix well. Pack in pint jars and store in refrigerator. Keeps for at least 6 months.

Serve with beef, pork, ham loaf, or hamburgers.

– Kathryn Light, Palmyra, PA

Pumpkin Cabbage Salad
Japan

Serves 6

Mix and set aside for 1-2 hours:
  2 c. cabbage, chopped
  ¹/₂ - 1 t. salt
Cook until crisp tender, then cool:
  2 c. squash, cubed
At the end of two hours squeeze excess moisture out of the cabbage. Mix cabbage and squash with enough mayonnaise to hold together.

Serve chilled.

This salad has colorful eye appeal and is nutritious.

– Mariko Kogoma, Tokyo, Japan

Nehemiah said, "Go and enjoy choice food and sweet drinks, and send some to those who have nothing prepared. This day is sacred to our Lord. Do not grieve, for the joy of the Lord is your strength."
– Nehemiah 8:10

Pattern of Family Meals

Traditionally the father eats first and is given the choice helpings of food. He is followed by the mother, with the children eating last. The father is called to the table by his wife kneeling in front of him and bowing her head. This is his signal that "Dinner is served!"

– Cindy Chisholm, Cumberland, MD (Macha, Zambia)

Rice and Raisin Salad
South Africa

Serves 8

Place in a large bowl and mix well, adding mayonnaise last:

> 3 c. cooked rice, cooled
> 1 small cabbage, grated
> 1 green pepper, diced
> 1 medium onion, diced
> $^1/_2$ c. raisins
> 1 c. mayonnaise

A nice change from the more usual cole slaw as rice gives the cabbage a milder flavor.

– Rosina Madlabane, Soshanguve, South Africa

40

Rice Salad
Québec

Salade de riz
(sa-LAHD doh REE)

Serves 6

Mix together:
   3/4 c. mayonaise
   6 t. lemon juice
   3/4 t. curry powder
   1 t. onion, finely chopped
   1/4 t. dry mustard
salt and pepper to taste
Add:
   3 c. rice, cooked and cooled
   1 1/2 c. celery, chopped
   1 1/2 c. cooked ham, cut into small cubes
   3/4 c. crushed pineapple, drained
Chill 4-6 hours.
Serve chilled salad on lettuce.

Brown rice makes a tasty substitute for white rice.

This is a popular item at our church potluck dinners.

– Lucie Boulanger, Romuald, Québec

Fresh Tomato Chutney
India

Tamatar Chatni
(Ta-MA-tar CHAT nee)

Serves 8-10

Chop:
   1 lb. tomatoes
   1 large onion
Add and mix well:
   2 dashes Tabasco sauce
   1/4 t. each salt and pepper
   1/2 t. sugar
   1/2 t. garlic powder
   dash of vinegar
Add:
   1 t. oil from mango pickle (or mustard or vegetable oil)

– A. J. Mann, Elizabethtown, PA (Bihar, India)

Taubolleh
Jordan

(Tah-BOO-lee)

Soak in 2 cups of water until soft (about 2 hours):
   1 c. bulgur wheat (medium crushed wheat)
Drain off excess water.
Combine in a bowl and add drained bulgur:
   1¹/₂ c. parsley, chopped very fine
   1 green onion, chopped in small pieces
   ¹/₂ c. mint leaves, chopped very fine
Combine and pour into the bulgur mixture,
mixing well:
   1 c. olive oil
   2 t. salt
   ¹/₂ c. lemon juice
Add:
   1 small tomato, chopped
Taubolleh is usually eaten by scooping up with a
lettuce leaf, cabbage leaf or vine leaf.

Options:
Reduce the amount of oil to ¹/₂ cup or add as
desired.
Use less parsley.
Add cucumber and garbanzo beans.

The above recipe as is, is much like the Mid-
Eastern recipes.

– Ethel Kreider, Lancaster, PA (Jordan)

Orange
Chutney
India

(Nah-RUN-gee
CHUT-nee)

About 4 cups

Mix all ingredients in a bowl:
   4 oranges, peeled, diced, and seeded
   1 onion, minced
   ¹/₂ c. grated coconut
   1 T. mint leaves, crushed
Cover and chill in refrigerator. Serve as an accompaniment to curry.

– Ken Hoke, Carlisle, PA (Bihar, India)

Raita
India

(RIE-tah)

About 4 cups

Peel, grate and set aside for 1 hour:
>   2 cucumbers

Mix:
>   1 medium onion, chopped fine
> $^1/_2$ t. ground cumin
>   1 pt. yogurt
> $^1/_2$ t. salt

Drain all water off cucumbers and add the yogurt mixture.

Serve as an accompaniment to curry.

– Ken Hoke, Carlisle, PA (Bihar, India)

Tomato Chutney
India

(Ta-MAH-tar CHUT-nee)

In blender grind:
>   1 lb. onions
>   2 oz. garlic
>   4 oz. fresh ginger
>   1 hot red pepper

In large kettle mix above together with:
>   4 lb. tomatoes, peeled and chopped
> $^3/_4$ c. slivered and blanched almonds
>   4 c. sugar
>   2 c. vinegar
>   2 t. salt

Toward end of cooking time add:
> $1^1/_2$ c. raisins

Cook, stirring frequently, until desired consistency (thick and syrupy). Seal in small canning jars.

Options: May use lesser amount of ginger and pepper. Especially delicious with curries but equally good as an accompaniment with any meat dish. Makes a nice hostess gift when sealed in a small jar and topped with a pretty bow!

– Leora Yoder, Mechanicsburg, PA (Bihar, India)

Chow Chow
Pennsylvania Dutch

Cook each vegetable separately until tender, not mushy:

> 2 qt. red, green and yellow peppers, diced
> 15-oz. can red kidney beans
> 1/2 pt. onions, chopped
> 2 qt. lima beans
> 2 qt. mix yellow and green beans, cut in 1/2-inch pieces
> 2 qt. carrots, diced
> 2 qt. celery, diced
> 1 1/2 qt. corn
> 1 qt. shell beans (lazy wife or soybeans)
> 2 qt. cauliflour florets

When each is cooked, drain hot water off and run cold water on vegetables to preserve color. Drain and layer in a large dish pan. Toss.
Add:

> 1 qt. sweet gherkin pickles

Have pint jars clean and fill each one to 1/2 inch from top.
Make the syrup and bring to a boil:

> 7 lb. sugar
> 3 pt. white vinegar
> 2 drops cinnamon oil

Pour into each jar to 1/2 inch from top. Seal. Process, boiling in water bath 15 minutes.

Serve with beef dinner.

I prepare these vegetables as they are ready in my garden and package them in the amount indicated in the recipe. This saves time. When fall comes this is the last thing I can. It's a lot of work but very rewarding.

– Mary Mylin, Willow Street, PA

What does a monkey know about the taste of ginger?

– Indian proverb

Esther's Chow Chow
Pennsylvania Dutch

Cook separately until tender:
- **2 lb. lima beans**
- **1 head cauliflour, cut into small pieces**
- **1 lb. carrots, sliced**

Put **1 head cabbage**, shredded, in canner; add salt and let stand for $1/2$ hour.

Add the cooked vegetables and the following ingredients to the cabbage and cook for 20 minutes:
- **2 stalks celery, diced**
- **5 c. onions, diced**
- **8 red and green peppers, diced**
- **6 green tomatoes, chopped**
- **12 cucumbers, sliced**
- **1 large can green beans**
- **cinnamon to taste**
- **celery seed to taste**
- **$8^1/_4$ c. sugar**
- **1 pt. vinegar**
- **1 T. tumeric mixed with a little vinegar**
- **small jar mustard**

Put in jars while hot and seal.

Can be used as a relish for dinner or for a picnic.

This is my aunt's recipe. As a child, it was fun to go to her "truck patch" to get the vegetables to make this.

– Marian Stone, Bainbridge, PA

Bless, O Lord, this food to our use, and consecrate us to thy service, and make us ever mindful of the needs of others, through Jesus Christ our Lord. Amen

– Common Prayer Book, Canada

Grandma Lilley's Sweet Red Beets
Pennsylvania Dutch

Wash but do not peel:
  5 lb. fresh beets
Leave ¹/₂ to 1 inch of the tops on each, so the juice does not bleed.
Cover with water and boil until tender. Drain, reserving 1 c. beet liquid.
Peel beets, leave whole or slice.
Heat the following in a kettle and heat until the sugar is dissolved:
  1. c. beet liquid
  2 c. water
  1 c. sugar
  1 c. cider vinegar
  3 t. salt
  1¹/₂ t. pepper
Add beets. Bring to a boil and boil 2 minutes.
Pack in jars and seal.
Marinate hard cooked peeled eggs in the red beet juice for 24 hours. If the eggs are peeled and dropped into the juice while hot, they will absorb the color and flavor better.

This is a good dish to serve with chicken corn soup and sandwiches. Red beet eggs make a light evening meal. When serving place whole beets, if small, with eggs on your serving dish. Cut some eggs in half. Makes a colorful dish.

When we have family picnics we always have fresh red beet eggs, homemade potato salad, hamburgers, etc., but the eggs are good with any meal.

– Mary Mylin, Willow Street, PA

He will also send you rain for the seed you sow in the ground, and the food that comes from the land will be rich and plentiful. In that day your cattle will graze in broad meadows.

– Isaiah 30:23

14-Day Pickles
Pennsylvania Dutch

Pack in a large 5 gal. crock and cover with salt brine strong enough to float an egg (about 1 c. **pickling salt in 3 gal. water**):
  50 slender, burpless cucumbers
Soak for 7 days.
Days 7-8: Drain and cover with boiling water for 34 hours.
Day 9: Drain and cut into ¹/₂ inch chunks. Cover with fresh boiling water and:
  2 T. alum
  5 oz. jar horseradish.
Day 10: Drain and cover with boiling water. Let stand overnight, then drain.
Dissolve sugar in vinegar over low heat:
  12 c. sugar
  1 qt. white vinegar
Prepare 2 spice bags (old sheet square will do) containing:
  2 t. whole cloves
  2 t. celery seeds
  2 sticks cinnamon
Place spice bags in among the cucumbers and pour syrup over them. To keep pickles down in syrup, place a plate over top of the pickles.
Days 11-14: Next day pour off syrup and bring to boil and pour back on pickles.
Repeat this four days.
Pack pickles in jars. Heat syrup to boiling point, pour over pickles and seal jars.

While living in Canada, I made these cucumber pickles and sold them as a Pennsylvania Dutch specialty. They sold very well at a very good price.

– Anna Ruth Ressler, Elizabethtown, PA

Oriental Dressing
Japan

Combine equal parts of:
- **sesame oil**
- **vinegar**
- **soy sauce**

I use this dressing with a variety of ingredients such as salads and chilled Chinese noodles. My friends of many nationalities like the flavor.

– Mariko Kogoma, Tokyo, Japan

Dutch Cupboard Salad Dressing
Pennsylvania Dutch

Fry **4 slices bacon** until crisp. Remove bacon from pan.
Into the drippings, add and cook slowly until thick:
- **$^1/_2$ c. sugar**
- **$^1/_2$ t. salt**
- **1 T. cornstarch**
- **1 egg, well beaten**
- **$^1/_4$ c. cider vinegar**
- **1 c. water**

Alternative: Omit bacon and cook all other ingredients, using 2 T. oil. While still warm add bacon bits.

Excellent on tossed salad or on lettuce alone.

– Millie Sollenberger, Hagerstown, MD

A man does not live on bread alone; he needs buttering up once in awhile.

– Good Things for Your Table
from Wainfleet Brethren in Christ Women.

GREECE

Most of the Greek village people had meat twice a year, lamb at Easter and pork at Christmas. Beef was a rare specialty. Pelleya, a village farmer, was our helper in the unit house. She enjoyed cooking with the MCC canned beef which she used in preparing moussaka. In spite of the eggplant flavor of the moussaka, it is a mild dish with a fluffy layer on the top. It was a special treat when served to the PAX team. I have memories of sitting in the village coffenias, under a huge tree. Moussaka was served with a salad which included feta cheese and ripe olives. Donkeys brayed in the background. I can still hear their sound which always reminded me of a rusty pump. The artesian wells were bubbling, bringing the cool fresh water to the village. The young men from the village danced as we enjoyed our food.

The Greek festival of the local Greek Orthodox Church (Camp Hill, PA) is the highlight of my current years. I attend to get the authentic Greek food and watch the young people perform the authentic dances. It feels like I have gone "home." The ladies of this church helped me perfect my recipe for moussaka .

– Beulah Heisey, Messiah Village, PA (MCC Greece)

R ecently we spent a week at the Mtshabezi Mission attending the Brethren In Christ Men's Retreat as well as teaching at a rural pastors' conference. There were about 200 men present. At one point in the meetings all of the men left the church building and took a walk out into the bush. We came to a clearing where some of the younger men had started a fire and slaughtered a young bull. The entire group sat on the ground; the speaker began to teach. Strips of meat were roasted on a grill which was simply an old bed frame. The meat was served to the men along with salt, as the teaching time and discussion continued. The meeting of men around the sharing of meat is something intrinsic to Ndebele culture. Sharing during our times of discussion was rich as well as helpful for me in better understanding and appreciating the African mind.

– *Dale Brantner, Bulawayo, Zimbabwe*

Vegetables

VEGETABLES

"Let the land
produce
vegetation"

—Gen. 1:11

Cultures that obtain most of their vegetables and fruits at the grocery store, fruit stand or supermarket lose the intimacy with the land and its edible vegetation that many others in primarily agrarian societies still have. This intimate knowledge of the land has, for example, helped many people know where to look in the wild for edible greens to cook and eat as a side dish to accompany the basic diet of carbohydrates. Such knowledge is particularly important when the rains don't come, regular crops fail, and what survives are often the plants that have grown wild for thousands of years. As cultures rely more on technology and cultivated farming, the knowledge of the elders may be lost without intentional efforts to pass it on to succeeding generations.

Vegetables can sometimes seem to be luxuries in a diet—side dishes that are nice colorful accompaniments but perhaps not as necessary to survival as the staples of rice, grain, beans and meat. At the same time, conventional wisdom is coming down more and more in favor of the health and disease-prevention benefits of eating vegetables.

While simple steamed vegetables with very little seasoning often go well as low-fat accompaniments to the main entrée, they certainly don't have to be served that way. In countries like India, where meat-eating is prohibited or restricted by religious belief, vegetables are never bland but become the basis for the "art of spice mixing." In fact, vegetarianism—often religiously based— has contributed to creativity in cooking, as cooks all over the world figure out tasty ways to serve vegetables as main rather than side dishes. Along with rice, beans and grains, vegetables are also lower on the food chain and don't require nearly as many resources and energy to produce as meats, especially beef.

When you prepare the recipes in this section, think about the people who have worked hard to till the land and grow the vegetables. Think about the effort it takes to produce a crop of corn or cucumbers or tomatoes. Think about the increasing loss of land to development and environmental problems and what that will mean to future generations. Think about how you can pass on a respect for and a sense of responsibility to care for the land that God created to produce vegetation.

Mushrooms with Peanut Butter
Zimbabwe

Serves 6

Cook together:
  4 c. fresh mushrooms, washed and sliced
  ¹/₂ c. water
  ¹/₂ t. salt
Set mushrooms aside.
Add to the water in which mushrooms were cooked:
  ¹/₂ c. peanut butter
Cook until thickened. Add the cooked mushrooms and simmer a few minutes longer. Serve with thick corn meal porridge or rice.

– Abbie Dube, Bulawayo, Zimbabwe

Howard Sikwela served as pastor at Choma Secondary School. He and his wife Christine invited me to their home for a farewell meal two days before I was to leave Zambia. I would have been happy for Tonga chicken and insima, but instead Christine had prepared meat balls in a delightful sauce served on rice. Vegetables, lemonade, cake and tea rounded out a wonderful menu. The expense involved in putting together such a meal was a tangible expression of the Sikwelas' friendship.

– John Long, Hopewell, PA (Choma, Zambia)

Praise be to Thee, my Lord, for our sister Mother Earth, who nourishes and sustains us all, bringing forth diverse fruits and many-colored flavors and herbs.

– St. Francis of Assisi

53

Gazpacho
Spain

Salsa
(Gahth-PAH-choh)

Serves 8

Chop in electric blender:
> 6 large ripe tomatoes
> 1 small clove garlic

Add to above mixture and blend again:
> $^1/_2$ onion
> $^1/_4$ green pepper
> $^1/_2$ cucumber

Strain mixture into tureen or serving bowl and chill in refrigerator.

Before serving, blend the following ingredients and add to the first mixture:
> 6 T. olive oil
> 4 T. lemon juice
> salt and pepper to taste
> 1$^1/_2$ c. tomato juice

Gazpacho is traditionally served accompanied by small bowls of raw vegetables and garlic croutons.

– Merly Bundy, Madrid, Spain

Hominy in Peanut Butter Sauce
Zimbabwe

Serves 2-4

Heat:
> 16-oz. can hominy, undrained

Add slowly and mix well:
> $^1/_4$ c. peanut butter

Simmer on very low heat for several minutes. May be served as the main course of a meal.

– Beatrice Ncube, Dekezi, Zimbabwe

Give me nothing but vegetables to eat and water to drink.

– Daniel 1:12

Tomato-Onion Relish
Honduras

Chilmol
(Chee-MOL)

Serves 10

Chop well and mix together:
10 tomatoes
3-4 onions
1 clove garlic
4 sweet bell peppers
3 mint leaves
juice of 1-2 lemons (or vinegar)
salt to taste

Common in restaurants as well as at home, this is good on meats, mixed with rice, in a tortilla, as well as a dip for tortilla chips. Keeps well in refrigerator.

– Yolanda Calderón de Herrera, Tegucigalpa, Honduras

Vegetable Pulau
Nepal

Serves 6

Soak **2 c. rice** in water for 2 hours.
In heavy saucepan heat for 1 minute:
1 T. oil
1 whole black cardamom
$1/2$ t. chili powder
$1/2$ t. ground cumin
Add and sauté, stirring frequently until golden:
1 med. size onion, chopped
1-inch piece fresh ginger root, chopped
Set aside spices and onions and add the drained rice to the oil that remains in pan. Toast until lightly browned.
Add and cook slowly for about 20 minutes:
4 c.water
When rice is nearly soft, add:
1-2 c. fresh or frozen peas
$1/2$ t. salt
Serve warm with chicken or meat curry.

– Esther Lenhert, Kathmandu, Nepal

Mole de Platano
California
Hispanic

Toast the following together:
> 1/2 oz. sesame seed
> 1 stick cinnamon or 1 t. ground cinnamon
> 3 whole cloves or 1/8 t. ground cloves
> 3 slices bread

Put in blender and blend with:
> 2 cooked tomatoes

Fry this mixture with a little oil. Add water so that the sauce is not too thick.
Add:
> sugar to taste
> 1 oz. melted chocolate

Peel, slice and fry in oil:
> 4 ripe plantain (cooking) bananas

Add cooked bananas to chocolate mixture and boil two or three minutes. Serve.

– Maria Arias, Cristo La Roca Church, Ontario, CA

Cabbage with Peanut Butter
Zimbabwe

Serves 6

Simmer for 5-10 minutes only:
> 1/2 head cabbage, medium-size, chopped
> 1/2 c. water
> 1/2 t. salt

Add by the tablespoon, mixing well after each addition:
> 1 c. peanut butter

Allow to simmer a few minutes. Serve with thick corn meal porridge.

In most African countries, the staple food is thick porridge made from corn meal. It is always served with relish made from a variety of fresh or dried vegetable leaves, such as pumpkin or wild vegetable leaves. Mushrooms, beans, meat, and sour milk are also used for relishes.

– Ardis Thuma, Bradford, Ohio

Cabbage Peanut Relish
Zambia

Serves 4

I volunteered to provide the "relish" for meals during a marriage enrichment seminar at our college in order to spare the students the cost of the most expensive part of the meals. As I realized that I could not afford to provide meat for all the meals and I was doubtful of my ability to make the kinds of vegetable relishes they enjoyed, I took my dilemma to the Lord in prayer, and the recipe above came to my mind. I served it to the students and was amazed at their appreciative comments. Some even asked for the recipe! We all thanked the Lord for his wisdom and provision for us.

In a skillet heat 2 T. cooking oil. Stir-fry, adding one vegetable at a time:
  1/2 c. onion, sliced
  3 c. cabbage, chopped
  3/4–1 c. tomato, diced
Add and warm thoroughly:
  1/2–1 t. salt
  few shakes pepper
  1/4 c. peanut butter*

*In Zambia I grind dried groundnuts (peanuts) with oil in the blender and then slow-fry the resulting paste, salting it as it fries. I then use this paste in the recipe above. Serve with insima (stiff cornmeal porridge) or rice as a main meal with or without an accompanying meat dish.

Options:
Use less cooking oil.
Increase amount of peanut butter to taste.
Add 1 green pepper, diced, with other vegetables.
Add 1 cup milk to make a sauce.

Relish is the term used for meat and/or vegetable dishes served with insima in Zambia. Any left-over peanut butter relish may be added to 1 or 2 cups milk and used as peanut butter soup for lunch the next day.

A similar Tonga recipe was submitted by Moono Anitah Chali, Mizinga Village, Choma, Zambia. She comments that it is tasty served in the Zambian cold season, June, July, August.

– Kathy Stuebing, Ndola, Zambia; Moono Anitah Chali, Choma, Zambia; Anna Graybill, Hershey, PA (Zambia); Ardys Thuma, Bradford, OH (Zambia)

The Sweet Potato Caper

An embarrassing "faux pas" over a sweet potato? Hardly! It was our first Christmas dinner at Barjora with our new friends, about forty members of the local Anglo-Indian community. The ladies had planned carefully; it wasn't easy with so many of the usual things not available. Fortunately, though, this was the sweet potato season, the small white variety, plentiful and cheap.

The anticipation of good food usually inspires light-hearted conversation and this occasion was no exception. It was a special "fun time" and happy smiles greeted the call to come to the table. But soon the mood seemed to change— it was just a little too quiet. And why were the sweet potato dishes still full? Little did we realize that we had placed our guests in a nearly impossible position. To eat the potatoes would have astounded the two servants who accompanied them and degraded them in the eyes of their village neighbors as the word got around. Yet would the missionaries not be offended if the potatoes were ignored entirely? The compromise was to eat only a tiny amount.

Later we learned that sweet potatoes were considered poor man's food. In the part of India where we lived, few people recognized as having any significant social status in the community would be seen eating, much less serving, sweet potatoes. And it is not improbable that our innocent "faux pas" would have been viewed by some villagers as a calculated insult to our guests.

– Phyllis and Arthur Pye, Ridgeville, ON
(Bihar, India)

Each year at the end of the third school term a farewell party is held for the graduating Grade 12 students of the Brethren in Christ fellowship at Choma Secondary School. The event is free for the graduates, while the other students must pay a modest fee. The Brethren in Christ teachers and headmaster are also invited. The meal is a feast by anyone's standards. Simple gifts are given to each graduate and each is given opportunity to say farewell to the fellowship.

– John Long, Hopewell, PA (Choma, Zambia)

Sauerkraut Pennsylvania Dutch

Makes 3 quarts

Combine:
1 large head of cabbage, shredded
2 T. salt
Let stand for 1 hour.
Stamp or squeeze cabbage with hands until brine appears.
Pack into quart jars being sure there is brine on the top.
Do NOT turn lids tight.
Let stand (somewhere out of smelling distance) for 3 or 4 days.
As cabbage "works" some of the juice may run out.
Fill up jars with boiling water (if necessary) and seal.

Boil or bake with pork and serve with mashed potatoes.

A good way to use those cabbage heads about to split in your garden.

– Millie Sollenberger, Hagerstown, MD

59

Cabbage Curry
India

Gobi Torkari
(Goh-bee TOHR-
kah-ree)

Serves 6

Shred coarsely:
>   2 lb. firm white cabbage
Heat and sauté until golden brown:
>   1¹/₂ T. butter
>   1 small onion, thinly sliced
Add to above:
>   1 t. salt
>   ¹/₂ t. black pepper
>   1 t. turmeric
Add cabbage and mix well. Cook uncovered over medium heat until cabbage shrinks enough to cover with lid (about 15 minutes).
Add:
>   1 t. lemon juice
Cover and cook until excess liquid is absorbed (about 1 hour). Uncover and add:
>   1 T. vegetable oil
Fry until thoroughly dry. Add and continue cooking for another 5 minutes:
>   2 t. curry powder
Serve as a main dish for a vegetarian meal or as a side dish with a meat curry and hot, fluffy rice.

– Ken Hoke, Carlisle, PA (Bihar, India)

Fresh Greens with Peanut Butter
Zambia

Lupusi
(Loo-poo-see)

Zimbabwe
Isitshebo
(Eh-say-CHAY-boh)

Serves 6

Cook for 20 minutes or until soft:
>   10 oz. fresh or frozen greens (chard, spinach, kale, etc.)
>   1 small tomato, chopped
>   1 c. water
>   ¹/₄ t. salt
Add by the tablespoon, mixing well after each addition:
>   ¹/₂ c. peanut butter
Allow to simmer a few minutes. Serve with thick corn meal porridge.

– Mrs. Sharoty Hansumo Chiswakama, Mwanambia, Zambia; Abbie Dube, Bulawayo, Zimbabwe

60

Cauliflower and Potato Curry
India

Alu Gobi ki Subzi
(AH-loo goh-bee kee SUB-zee)

Serves 6

Sauté in 2 T. hot vegetable oil:
  2 t. ground coriander
  $1/4$ t. chili powder
  $1/4$ t. turmeric
Add and sauté for a minute or two:
  1 T. green pepper, finely chopped
  1 medium onion, finely chopped
Mix in:
  1 medium cauliflower cut in 1-inch pieces
  3 potatoes, quartered
  1 t. salt
  $1/8$ t. black pepper
Add just enough water to cook vegetables. Cover and cook until water has evaporated.
Sprinkle with **1 T. lemon juice** and serve.

Serve with rice or chapatis.

– Gulabi McCarty, Ridgeway, ON (Delhi, India)

Cabbage and Pea Curry
India

Mattar Gobi
(MAH-ter goh-bee)

Serves 6

Heat in a heavy skillet:
  3 T. vegetable oil
Add and sauté:
  1 medium onion thinly sliced or chopped
  2 t. cumin powder
  $1/2$ t. turmeric
Add and stir until coated:
  $1/2$ head of cabbage, thinly sliced
  $1/2$ c. water (enough to cook thoroughly)
  1 t. salt
  pinch of black pepper
Add, after about 20 minutes slow cooking:
  $1/2$ cup tomato or V-8 juice
  10 oz. frozen peas
Cook about ten minutes longer.
Serve as vegetable with rice.

– Gulabi McCarty Ridgeway, ON (Delhi, India)

Henry Hostetter served for many years as secretary of the Foreign Mission Board (now Board for World Missions). He recalls a Christmas he spent in India in 1948. A youth committee had been appointed by General Conference in 1933. Later this committee raised money to send personnel overseas. Henry Hostetter and Graybill Wolgemuth were the two General Conference appointees to visit the Africa and India fields in 1938.

World War II intervened so it was not until May 1948 when they actually set sail. December found them still in Nairobi, their plans stalled by a delayed ship. How could they get to India in time to celebrate Christmas with the missionaries as they had promised to do? So they wouldn't disappoint the missionaries, their only alternative was to travel by air in a 22-passenger DC-3, "the latest" in technology at that time but truly a novel experience for rural Pennsylvanians. The flight took them to Addis Ababa, then the Arabian Peninsula and finally, in the same plane, to Calcutta, a long flight of 11 hours as the pilot sought to evade a cyclone.

And what does Henry remember of that Christmas? The privilege of joining the missionary family to celebrate Christmas at an Anglo-Indian home near Barjora. He remembers the invitation to sit down on the grass in the warm December sunshine where, for the first time in his life, he was served rice and curry on a banana leaf and was expected to eat with his fingers. He found the food not too hot or spicy but he did not join others who added hot peppers to their curry and ate with tears running down their cheeks.

Henry sensed a very congenial fellowship in that setting as hospitality and love were shared with North Americans far from home at Christmas.

– Henry Hostetter, Messiah Village, PA

Fried Cauliflower
Egypt

Arnabeet
(Ar-nah-BEET)

Serves 6–8

Cut **1 cauliflower** into flowerets and steam (or microwave) until tender. Don't overcook—it should retain shape. Drain.
Beat with a fork:
   2 eggs
Add:
   1 t. salt
   3 t. cumin
   6 cloves garlic, mashed
      (put in small plastic bag and roll with rolling pin or use garlic press)
   2 T. flour
If too thick add water so it is runny but thicker than gravy.
Dip each floweret into mixture and fry in deep oil until golden in color.

– Amal, Egypt

S ince I quite enjoy trying unusual foods, I had lots of opportunities for tastebud adventures in China. Our Chinese friends made tasty vegetable dishes by frying leafy branches of a particular tree, or by coating lilac blossoms with a flour and water mixture and steaming them (very fragrant tasting). In meats, the Chinese eat almost any part of an animal. Chewy chicken feet and slippery pork tendons are among the more popular choices. At banquets, we ate the specialties that could really make news to write home about – like dog meat (the Chinese even have a famous dish called "dragon and tiger" made from snake and dog meat); or little frogs (deep fried and crunchy); cicadas; and even scorpions (also deep fried and tasting a little like potato chips)!

– Joyce Peterman,
Manheim, PA

Egg and Spinach Stirfry
China

Serves 3-4

Heat in large skillet or wok:

2 T. oil (peanut or soybean preferred but may use any oil)

Add and sauté lightly:

2 cloves garlic, crushed or chopped fine
1 med. onion, chopped

When onions begin to soften, add and stir constantly (as if for scrambled eggs):

5 eggs, beaten

When eggs are cooked, remove mixture from wok. Rinse the wok, dry well, and again add and heat:

2 T. oil

To hot oil, add and stir constantly:

1 lb. fresh spinach, torn into small pieces

(water on spinach leaves will make a little liquid, or you might add a little water). When the spinach gets limp, add:

egg and onion mixture
$^1/_2$–1 t. salt
$^1/_2$–1 t. soy sauce (optional)
$^1/_4$–$^1/_2$ t. sesame oil (optional)

Serve over steamed, fried rice. Mixture is flavorful, but you may want to have soy sauce available to add to the flavor.

Spinach and many other vegetables are abundant and cheap at the open air markets in China. This dish is typical of everyday fare. By contrast, when entertaining guests, our Chinese friends tried to use more meat dishes. They also often prepared the same basic egg and vegetable dish but used tomato wedges or chopped cucumbers instead of spinach.

– Joyce Peterman, Lancaster, PA

Colorblind

We lived in Zambia for ten years and both of our children were born there. One day when Joshua was about four years old we were eating lunch with Maureen, the girl who helped care for the children. We were talking about people being different and Maureen asked Joshua who at the table was different. He looked around and could not see anyone who was different. We told him to keep looking. He came up with the fact that Mom, Tabitha, and Maureen were girls and he and Dad were boys! Then Maureen pointed out that her skin color was different. He had not even noticed or thought that it was something worth mentioning!

*– Ann Marie Parry,
Danville, PA,
(Choma, Zambia)*

Tomato Sauce
India

Serves 6

Sauté lightly in $^1/_2$ T. **salad oil** :
   $^1/_2$ **medium onion, chopped**
Add:
   3-4 large tomatoes, peeled and quartered
When tomatoes are soft, add:
   3 T. sugar
   $^1/_4$ **t. salt**
Serve warm with rice or pasta.

– Saroj Murmu, Madhipura, Bihar

In order to pronounce English, "we need a hot potato in the mouth."
– Colombian Saying

Sweet Potato Cakes
Zimbabwe

Serves 6

Cook and mash:
    1 large sweet potato
Add and mix thoroughly:
    1 egg
    1 T. sugar
    ¹/₂ c. flour
    1 T. melted margarine
    ¹/₄ t. salt
    1 t. lemon juice and rind (optional)
    ¹/₄ c. milk, if needed

Heat **2 T. oil** in skillet and fry until nicely browned on both sides.

– Jeste Mlilo, Bulawayo, Zimbabwe

Isitshwala

Isitshwala is a staple food for Zimbabwe. It is a thick porridge made from ground corn. It can be served with sour milk, a variety of fresh or dried vegetables as well as with meat. It is thoroughly enjoyed by most locals and many people eat it two or three times a day.

In a home setting, when a young man marries, one of the things looked forward to by the whole extended family is the new bride's cooking. When neighbors and friends greet members of this family they make reference to the joy of having "new isitshwala" which really implies a new cook in the homestead. Over the years the term "isitshwala" has become synonymous with a new bride. Thus people will greet or congratulate each other by saying "Sesibonga isitshwala esitsha," meaning "How we appreciate the new bride!"

This does not in any way imply that the bride is appreciated only for the anticipated work she will do but also that she is valued highly.

– Doris Dube, Bulawayo, Zimbabwe

After Bishop and Mrs. Jake Shenk stepped into the bishop's office they made an effort to visit as many congregations as possible in all the five church districts. As would be expected, in true African style they have been treated to all sorts of dishes. Their response to such hospitality demands that they eat whatever is placed before them.

Bishop Shenk tells of a day in Gokwe when he had three breakfasts, and yet there was another day when he was served even more food. He was being hosted by the Bhebhes. When he got to the church for the service there were no people present so the service was delayed slightly. He was served half a melon to eat while he waited. The service finally took place at 3:00 pm. Afterwards there was some discussion with the members before he made his way back to the Bhebhe's village.

There the bishop was served a big bowl of peanuts. Since he imagined that this was going to be his supper, he really ate his fill of them. As soon as he was finished with this, tea and bread were brought. He thought that surely this must be the evening meal and he ate and drank. No sooner had he finished, then isitshwala, (corn meal porridge) and chicken were brought in together with a plateful of goat meat. By that time he was really full but still he ate on. They had evening prayers at Nsingo's village. As they headed back to Bhebhe's village, the bishop was thinking of retiring for the night, but no sooner had he arrived than he was served a bowl of rice and chicken. Of course he ate that too, thus bringing to an end, a very satisfying day!

– Doris Dube, Bulawayo, Zimbabwe

Cooked Dried Corn
Pennsylvania Dutch

Serves 6

Soak for 1 hour in warm water to cover:
   2 c. dried sweet corn
Cook corn until soft and the water is almost absorbed.
Stir in and bring to a boil:
   1 t. salt
   2 t. sugar
   1/2 c. cream or sweet milk

– Arlene Martin, Elizabethtown, PA

Creamed Potatoes Colombia

Papas Chorriadas
(PAH-pahs Chore-e-AH-dahs)

Serves 4-6

In a large saucepan add and cook:
1 T. oil
1 large onion, chopped fine
4-5 medium tomatoes, peeled and chopped
Add:
1 c. water
1 t. salt
dash pepper
1 T. margarine
2 lb. medium potatoes, peeled and
    quartered
Cook until potatoes are soft but not mushy.
In a jar with lid, shake until smooth:
1/2 c. flour
1 c. milk
Pour into the tomato-potato mixture, stirring and cooking until thickened. Pour into serving dish and top with grated cheese. Serve with rice and meat.

– Gloria de Silva, Bogota, Colombia

Corn Pie Pennsylvania Dutch

Serves 6

Line a 9-inch pie plate with:
1/2 of 2-crust pie dough.
Fill with:
2 c. fresh corn cut from cob
1/2 c. milk
1 T. butter
2 t. salt
1 t. sugar
1 hard-boiled egg
Arrange hard-boiled egg slices over top.
Cover with top crust. Pierce with fork.
Bake at 325 degrees for 25 minutes or longer.
Serve hot with main course.

– Dorothy Ebersole, Cleona, PA

Shoe Peg Corn Casserole
Southern United States

Serves 10

Combine:
   15-oz. can French style green beans
   8-oz. container sour cream
     (non-fat may be used)
   $10^3/_4$-oz. can cream of celery soup
   $^1/_2$ c. diced Velveeta cheese
   $^1/_4$ c. onion, chopped
   $^1/_4$ c. bell pepper, chopped
   2 11-oz. cans shoe peg corn
Place in 9 x 13-inch ungreased casserole.
Mix together and top with:
   $1^1/_2$ c. crushed Ritz crackers
   4 T. melted margarine
Bake at 325° for 45 minutes.

– Pat Rubley, McMinnville, TN

Eggplant in Tomato Sauce
Egypt

Betengan
(BEH-ten-gun)

Fry sliced eggplant in 1-2 T. butter or oil.
Salt to taste.
Sauce:
Sauté in 2 T. oil:
   1 T. minced garlic
Add:
   3 medium tomatoes, chopped
Simmer 5 minutes.
Add fried eggplant and simmer for 2-3 minutes.
Serve with pita bread.

– Brian and Marcelle Zook, Egypt

Then God said, "I give you every seed–bearing plant on the face of the whole earth and every tree that has fruit with seed in it. They will be yours for food."

– Gensis 12:9

Vegetable Pancake
Japan

Okonomiyaki
(Oh-koh-no-mee-YAH-kee)

Combine for batter:
> 1 c. flour
> 1 egg plus water to make 1 c.
> ¹/₄ t. salt
> dash monosodium glutamate (optional)

Prepare a combination of chopped
> vegetables such as **onions, carrots,
> green peppers, cabbage, mushrooms,
> bean sprouts,** for a total of approximately
> 3 cups.

Sauté ¹/₄ lb. any meat such as **sausage,
hamburger, squid, etc.**

Mix all together and fry in pan like a pancake,
using 1-2 T. oil.

Pancakes may be topped with **dried fish flakes or
sea weed flakes.**

Serve with a sprinkling of soy sauce.

– Elaine Wright, Okinawa, Japan

Squash Puppies
Southern United States

Mix:
> 1¹/₂ c. self-rising* cornmeal
> ¹/₂ c. self-rising* flour
> ¹/₂ t. soda

Drain and mash:
> 1 c. tender yellow squash, cooked

Mix with:
> 1 egg, beaten
> 3 T. onions, chopped (optional)
> 1 c. buttermilk

Add to dry ingredients.

Drop from teaspoon into hot oil and fry.

Cook until golden brown.

Remove from fat and drain on absorbent
paper towel.

Serve hot with fish or whatever you wish.

*If using regular cornmeal and flour, add **2 t.
baking powder.**

– Tammie Burger, Smithville, TN

Squash Dressing
Southern United States

Serves 4–6

Cook and drain:
    2 c. yellow squash
Add:
    2 c. cornbread crumbs
    1 onion, chopped
    $^1/_2$ stick butter or margarine
    1 can condensed cream of mushroom soup
        (lowfat may be used)
    1 t. sugar
    1 t. sage
Mix well, then add:
    1 egg, beaten
Mix thoroughly.
Pour into baking dish and bake at 350° for 30 minutes.

Great for any occasion as a vegetable dish.

– Tammie Burger, Smithville, TN

Fried Plantain
Venezuela

Platanos fritos
(PLAH-tah-nos FREE-tos)

Use **ripe plantains (cooking bananas)** found in the fresh produce section of the supermarket, (they look longer and thicker than bananas). Cut off the peel, slice lengthwise and fry in a small amount of oil until nicely browned on both sides.

These can be part of any meal.

– Thata Book, Manheim, PA (Cagua, Venezuela)

Potato and Yogurt Curry
Nepal

(AH-loo or DAH-hee KAH-ree)

Serves 8

Cut into ¼-inch cubes:
   6 raw potatoes
Add:
   ¼ c. water
Cook slowly just until soft and almost dry.
In **2 t. hot oil** sauté until golden brown:
   1 medium onion, chopped
Add to above and fry for 2 minutes:
   ½ t. chili powder
   ½ t. ground cumin
   ½ t. turmeric
   ½ t. salt
Add hot potatoes and mix lightly with onions and spices.
Fold in:
   1 c. plain yogurt
Cover and heat through.

Serve when hot with rice or flat bread (chappati).

– Esther Lenhert, Kathmandu, Nepal

Potato seller

72

Meats

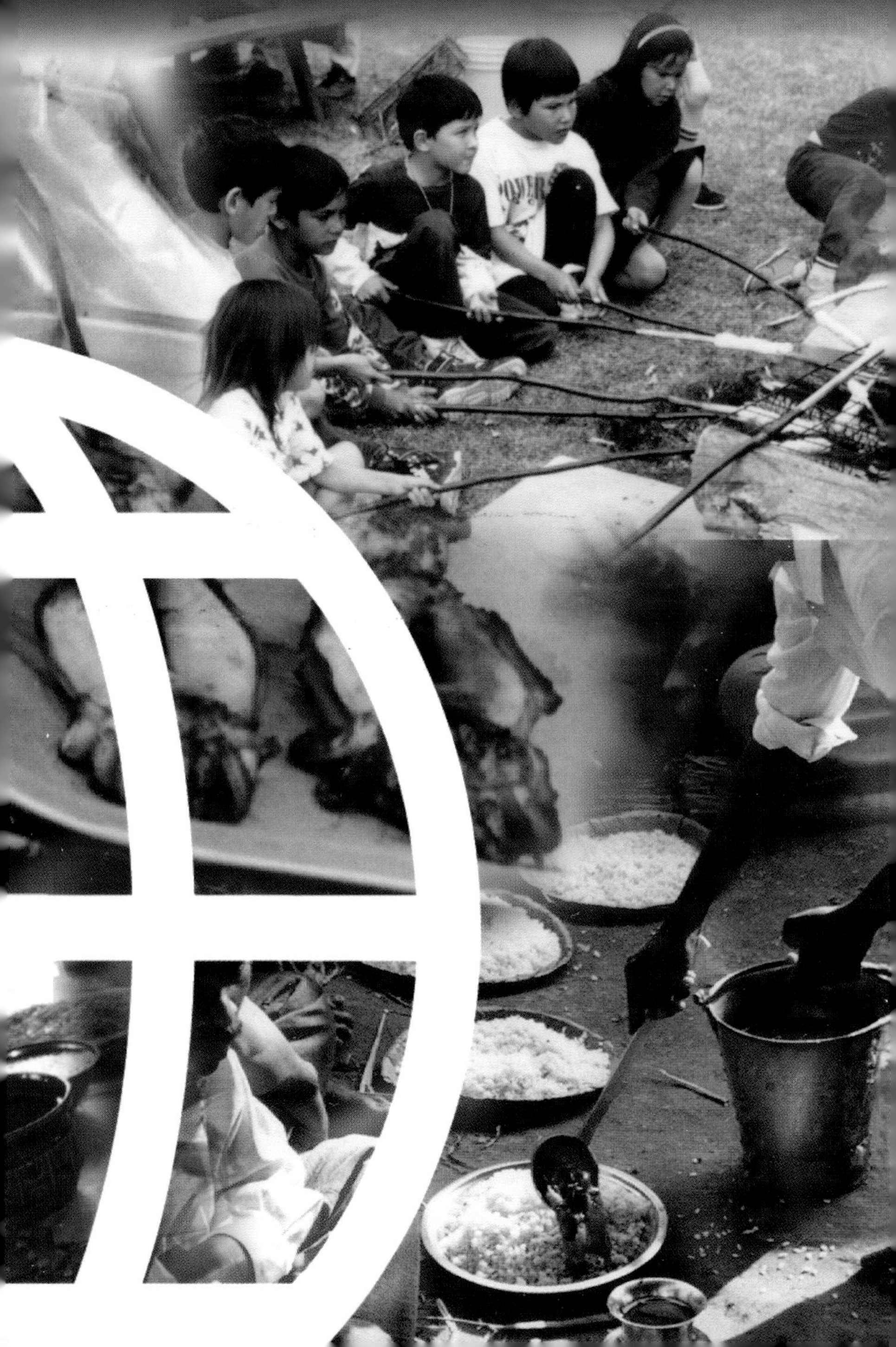

MEATS

When Esther and Mordecai's plan to rescue the Jews
from the evil plot of Haman to destroy them was
successful, the Jews were able "to get relief from their
enemies." The day on which this happened became "a day
of joy and feasting, a day for giving presents to each other"
to be celebrated annually from then on. What had started
out as a disastrous turn of events for the Jewish people
became a regular occasion for joyous feasting.

I observed something similar a number of years ago on
a visit to Zambia during a time of severe drought when
crops had failed and food was scarce. Many people told us
their stories of hardship. Maize was in short supply (in
fact, most of the maize that they were eating while we were
there had been shipped in from outside the country by
relief organiza-tions) and meat was a rare treat as an
accompaniment to their traditional insima.

One day we went out to the village of the headman at
Sikalongo Mission to visit and talk with him about how he
and his family were coping with the effects of the drought.
We sat around and visited while children were running
about playing; we walked out to look at the fields where
new maize was beginning to grow in expectation of rain
that year; we examined a grain storage system and listened
to the headman explain how it worked and how it might
help to prevent future grain shortages.

Meanwhile, the women were preparing a meal for their
guests. When we finally sat down to eat, we discovered that
they had killed a goat for us that day. In a time when food
was in short supply and what little wealth they had was in
livestock, they killed a goat and cooked and served it in
honor of their guests from the United States and to thank
us for the help that North Americans and others had given
them during their time of distress.

Meat dishes are common around the world, but they
are also often used sparingly in recognition of the
resources needed to produce meat and because meat is
often simply unavailable. Meat is saved for special
occasions, such as when the Jewish people celebrated their
victory over their enemies or Zambians wanted to be
hospitable to their guests and express their appreciation.

Christmas in India

Mary and I were living at Barjora, Bihar, in north India. It was the Christmas season and we had invited our Anglo-Indian neighbors from Dumaria to our home for Christmas dinner. The big question in Mary's mind was, "What shall I serve for dinner?" One choice would have been rice, lentils and curry but she knew her guests could make excellent Indian food so she wanted something different for this feast. She also knew that neither turkey nor chicken were available. She might have served fish but that also was unobtainable. Finally, instead of stuffing a turkey (as she would have done if at home in North America), she decided to have a goat killed and then stuff it. The butcher was called, the goat was in place, and the knife was poised—but....

Here I must retrace my steps to give some background. Some time earlier I had left my gun with my friend, Arthur Singh, so that he could, take it to the Supaul government office to renew my license. He promised to bring it to me at Barjora as soon as he could, but he also asked for some shells to do a little hunting before returning the gun. The evening before he planned to return the gun, he took a flashlight and the gun and went out into the jungle to look for wild game. Sure enough, a pair of eyes glowed in the dark and Arthur shot and killed a deer. The next day he was pleased to put a leg of venison on his bicycle and so he arrived at our home—just before the butcher killed the goat. Thus, we enjoyed a wonderful Christmas dinner with our Anglo-Indian friends of roast venison and all the wonderful things that Mary prepared to go with it.

But the story doesn't end there. Later that afternoon Arthur returned to Supaul only to find the village folk at his door asking why he had not brought the leopard home which he had shot the previous night. He informed them that it was a deer that he shot, but they insisted that there was a dead leopard lying in the jungle. Sure enough, to his surprise the leopard was lying just where he shot it. Probably the leopard pounced on the deer at the exact moment that Arthur shot, thus killing the two animals with one shot. Believe it or not, this is true—I saw that leopard with my own eyes!

– William R. Hoke, Mechanicsburg, PA (Bihar, India)

Cabbage and Beef Stew
Guyana

Serves 4

Dice and boil in 5 cups water for 20 minutes:
   1 lb. beef.
While meat cooks, cut into bite-size pieces and set aside:
   1¹/₂ lb. cabbage
In another container, place:
   1 medium tomato, chopped
   2 T. celery, chopped
   2 T. fresh scallions, chopped
   1 small onion, chopped
When meat has cooked, drain water and set aside.
Heat a little oil in skillet over low heat.
Add beef and chopped ingredients (not cabbage) to oil and cook for 2 minutes, stirring occasionally.
Add cabbage with **1 t. salt and dash of pepper.**
Cover and cook 15 minutes, stirring occasionally.
May add some of the reserved water during the cooking, if needed.

Serve with cooked rice for an evening meal.

– Rita Lutchman, Bronx, NY

Our Father, who art in heaven, hallowed be thy name.
Accept our gratitude for once again, giving us this day and
our daily bread. Amen.

– Common Prayer Book, Canada

Shredded Beef Nicaragua

Carne Desmenuzada
(CAR-nay Des-me-noo-SAH-dah)

Serves 6

Boil **1 lb. stewing beef** until tender with:
2-3 cloves garlic cut in half
¹/₂ t. salt
Allow to cool. With your fingers, pull meat into fine shreds.
Chop and fry together:
1 large onion
1 large green pepper
4 medium tomatoes
Add:
shredded beef
3 T. catsup
vinegar, as desired
salt, as desired
Boil together about 5 minutes.

Serve with rice and a salad of cabbage slaw, onion, and tomato. Carne desmenuzada can be prepared the day before and reheated. May offer hot sauce at the table.

– Perla Estrada, Managua, Nicaragua

I t was Christmas and our family's first experience of the annual village tour with the Santal Christians. Everywhere we went hospitality was offered, usually sweet, milky tea and rice puffed in sand. But at least once a day an entire meal of rice, lentils and vegetable curry was served. Then one day we stopped to sing, preach and pray at the Christian village of Sukhasin. And there, seated inside the family courtyard, we were feted to wonderful chicken curry.

But what was that curious specimen served on the senior missionary's plate? Could it possibly be . . . surely not . . . but it was . . . the entire head of the chicken offered as a gesture of respect. We inexperienced missionaries eagerly watched to see what our superintendent, Bill Hoke, would do. One minute the head was on his plate. The next it was gone – over the courtyard fence for the ever present village dogs! How could he be so disrespectful? It was a relief to learn that the host did not really expect the missionary would eat this morsel. It was a learning moment for the young missionary family – humor abounds in every culture.

– Erma J. Sider, Mechanicsburg, PA (Bihar, India)

Lancashire
Hot Pot
England

Serves 4

Put **2 lb. cubed beef** in a deep casserole and season with salt and pepper to taste.

Arrange the following ingredients in thin layers over the meat:

2 large onions, sliced
1 c. carrots, sliced
1¹/₂ lb. potatoes, sliced

End with a layer of potatoes arranged in overlapping slices.

Pour **1 c. beef stock** over the above ingredients and cover.

Put in 325° preheated oven. Cook for 2 to 2¹/₂ hours or until meat is tender.

Increase temperature to 400°F, uncover, and cook for 30 minutes or until top layer of potatoes is brown.

Great for evening meal.

– June Simmonds, London, England

Being an M.K. in India, as well as a missionary in Africa (both in Zimbabwe and Zambia), I have absorbed some of the delicious food of two continents. In India I learned these recipes as a child. I would squat around the fires with the Indian women and watch them as they cooked their food. Since in those early days I was the only white child for miles around, I think I had somewhat of a revered position. I was also, undoubtedly, an oddity. But I was usually rewarded with a small dish of the delicious curries and other goodies. "This," they would say, "is for Aides Baba (child)." Ardys was an impossible name for them to pronounce. I've also learned Indian cooking from both my mother and father. Dad is a great curry maker. There is usually a pot of his curry on the stove for my sisters and me when we come home!

– Ardys E. Thuma, Bradford, OH (Africa, India)

Beef Tongue in Sauce
Nicaragua

Lengua en Salsa
(LEHN-gua en SAL-sah)

Serves 10 or more

Wash the **tongue** in salt water. Place in a large pan and cover with water. Boil 2 to 3 hours until tongue is soft. Peel off the skin that covers the tongue and slice tongue.
Melt:
   $1/4$ c. margarine in large frying pan
Add:
   sliced tongue
   $1/3$ c. catsup
   $1/2$ t. salt
   pinch of sugar
   $1/2$ c. water
Cook for about 25 minutes on low heat, adding water as needed.
Serve on a platter. Garnish with:
   $1/2$ c. chopped celery on top of tongue
   $1/2$ c. cooked peas around the edges
   sliced olives, if you wish
   a couple of parsley sprigs in the corners

Serve with rice and a salad.

This recipe is made for special occasions or a special meal. It is not necessarily for holiday meals. It is special because it is expensive to make. Since it must boil so long, it uses a lot of gas or firewood.

– Martiza Mairena, Managua, Nicaragua

Moussaka
Greece

(moo-SA-kah)

Serves 8

Eggplant layer:
Peel and cut in $^1/_2$-inch slices:
   2 large or 3 small eggplants
Layer on a platter. Salt each layer lightly, if
desired. Cover with plastic wrap for 45 minutes
so moisture can be drawn out. Oil a 9x13-inch
casserole and place prepared eggplant slices on
bottom in a single layer. Bake in 450° oven for
8-10 minutes. Do not turn.
Meat mixture:
Sauté in **2 t. oil:**
   2 medium onions, chopped
   2 garlic buds, crushed
Add to the above and brown evenly:
   1$^1/_2$ lb. lean ground beef
   salt and pepper to taste
When browned, add and simmer gently until
liquid is absorbed:
   18 oz. can tomato paste
   $^1/_2$ c. water
   $^1/_4$ c. grated Parmesan cheese
Sauce:
In saucepan melt:
   6 T. butter or margarine
Add and stir until smooth:
   10 T. flour
Add gradually and stir constantly until thickened:
   4 c. warm milk (may use powdered milk)
Add, stirring until melted:
   1$^1/_2$ c. grated Parmesan cheese
Remove from heat. In mixing bowl, beat:
   6 eggs (or equivalent egg subtitue)
Add a little of the cooked sauce to eggs while
beating on low speed of mixer. Add eggs to sauce
in saucepan.
Spread meat mixture over eggplant which has
been removed from oven. Pour sauce over
eggplant and meat mixture. If desired, sprinkle
with cinnamon or nutmeg. Bake at 350° for one
hour. Allow to cool slightly. Cut into squares.

Serve with crusty bread and a Greek salad. A
popular Greek dish.

– Beulah Heisey, Mechanicsburg, PA (Greece)

Greek Hospitality

Although the Greek people live close to the soil in the mountain villages, food plays a very important part in their family life. Holidays are a time of real celebration as the women cook and cook while the men sit in the coffee shops playing games and talking.

Weddings and baptisms are a time of celebration. They make many sweets such as koulourakia, karidopita, kadaifi, baklava, and finikia. Liqueurs also are prepared and served to the guests. When guests come to the house they must be served Turkish coffee. This bitter-sweet thick coffee is prepared and served in tiny demitasse cups. A hostess would be very offended if a guest refused a cup of coffee. When I lived in Greece in the early sixties, it was not an easy task to prepare the coffee. I have even seen a ball of cotton lighted by fire to heat the coffee. It was a very humbling experience to know that the women had worked with such hardship to honor my presence in their home.

I felt that I had become a true friend when I was able to have my fortune told. The coffee cup is turned upside down. The thick grounds run to the saucer forming lines on the side of the cup. These lines indicate "a journey," "a letter," or "a sum of money will be coming" as my future is joyfully told. We laughed together and cried together as we shared this form of friendship.

Preserved fruits were also a symbol of friendship shared as we visited from house to house. These could be apple, quince, orange peel, cherries and strawberries — "spoon sweets" served to us. The sweets are served in a teaspoon on a small dish. They are sweeter than our jams. A glass of clear cold water is then offered following the eating of the sweet. Sometimes small candies are offered also.

When I returned to Greece for a visit years later, I wondered if this hospitality would still be a part of the culture. Many changes have come even to the mountain villages. Electricity is now installed in each home. Refrigeration and electric stoves are standard equipment in the majority of the homes. As my friend Lois and I returned to a remote village close to the Yugoslavian border, we were greeted with this same special offering of sweets, liqueurs and pastries. Friends dropped what they were doing to sit with us. We walked the dusty streets from house to house,

(continued on page 84)

greeting friends who gathered as we went to the different homes. Time stood still as we shared. We visited friends in the city and, there also, sweets and coffee were offered to us. We giggled as our fortunes were told. Of course, I was going to make a long trip!

We visited a friend in Aridea, the village center during my days with MCC. Here our special friend, Marika, served us fresh fruit, candy, sweets and coffee. Each item is savored separately and after fifteen to twenty minutes the next item is brought. In an unhurried way we shared together. Visiting an elderly couple in one of the larger towns we received the same hospitality. They were crippled and barely able to function in their own home but they so graciously shared with us what they had.

Not only did our Greek friends offer small treats but they also often prepared a sumptuous meal. To me this seemed a hardship but they did it so effortlessly and so graciously. Their encouraging word to us to eat, even when we were already filled with their delicious food, was "Fi! Fi!" (Eat! Eat!). I had gone to Greece to serve in the name of Christ. Frequently I felt that I was the one being served in the name of Christ by the many ways these people shared themselves.

– Beulah Heisey, Mechanicsburg, PA (Greece)

Meat Sauce with Egg
Egypt

Shakshouka
(Shuk-SHOO-kah)

Fry together:
  1 lb. ground beef
  2 onions, chopped
Add and cook:
  1 pepper, chopped
  2-3 tomatoes, chopped
  1 small can tomato sauce
  salt and pepper to taste
Break 1 egg in mixture and cook until set (cover and simmer, or put in oven for 5 minutes).
Serve with pita bread.

– Brian and Marcelle Zook, Egypt

Meatball Curry India

Beef Kofta
(GOHSHT KOHR-mah)

Serves 4-6

Mix:
1 lb. lean ground beef
1 onion, minced
6 cloves garlic, minced
1 T. Worcestershire sauce
2 t. marjoram
1 t. thyme
1 t. salt
1 T. curry powder
1 egg, beaten

The above ingredients constitute the basic seasoning for the meat, and while these meatballs can be used for hors d'oevres, as a side dish with curries, and for snacks, they can also be prepared as a curry. To prepare the meatballs, roll into balls of desired size and brown slowly.

To use the above for a curry:
Chop:
1 medium-size onion
Fry onion lightly in:
1 T. vegetable oil
1 t. ground ginger
Add to above and sauté for about 5 minutes:
1 t. turmeric
1 t. curry powder
1 t. salt
Add and stir so they are covered with spices:
4 potatoes, washed and cubed
Add to above:
$1/2$ lb. tomatoes, chopped
1 T. yogurt or lemon juice

Fry well for another 5-10 minutes, then add the meat balls, stir, and cover with:
2 c. hot water
Allow to simmer, stirring occasionally until potatoes are tender.
Serve with hot, fluffy rice.

– Ken Hoke, Carlisle, PA

Steak and Eggplant Stew
South Africa

Serves 6

Heat 1 T. oil in a large saucepan, add and braise lightly:

    1 large onion, chopped
    1 large eggplant, chopped
    1 lb. stewing beef coated with
    2 T. flour

Add:

    1 c. water
    1 c. uncooked rice
    1 16 oz. can crushed tomatoes
    1 t. salt
    1 beef bouillon cube
    $^1/_4$ t. cayenne pepper
    $^1/_2$ t. parsley
    $^1/_2$ t. coriander
    $^1/_2$ t. lemon dill
    $^1/_2$ t. garlic
    1 t. cilantro (coriander leaf)

Bring to a boil and simmer for 45 minutes to 1 hour, adding more water gradually as needed.

– Rosina Madlabane, Soshanguve, South Africa

I n times of drought the people of Zambia have very little to eat. They may not have relish (vegetable greens) or nshima (thick corn meal) which are the staples of their diet. Sometimes a family is out of food so relatives and friends will give them food to prevent starvation. When food gets scarce, the women are forced to go out in the bush to find edible leaves, flowers and fruit to supplement their diet. There is also a wild fruit that the people sometimes eat to help decrease their appetite.

– Ann Marie Parry,
Danville, PA
(Choma, Zambia)

"**R**ed mouth was killed by food" is a saying often made by people when they are at a feast and have overeaten but are still tempted to go on tasting more dishes.

A story is told of a Zulu warrior called Mlomo Obomvu (Red Mouth). There was inter-fighting between two Zulu regiments. The regiment to which Mlomo Obomvu belonged had made camp while resting from enemy attack. They had slaughtered the fattest of cows and a feast was about to begin. Suddenly a warning shout came from the sentinel, "The enemy is here." There was no time to stop and feast. Everyone fled.

Mlomo Obomvu, however, could not bear the thought of turning his back on all that food. He gathered his spears and really meant to follow the others but the aroma of roasting meat overpowered him. He stopped to eat a little from the nearest pot. Thus the enemy found him — still eating. They ran a spear through him. Thus Mlomo Obomvu died because of a great love for food.

– Doris Dube,
Bulawayo, Zimbabwe

Pan Sautéed Meat and Vegetables
Japan

Teppanyaki
(Tay-pahn-YAH-kee)

Quick fry meat and vegetables, in small amount of salad oil, in frying pan in center of table:
   1 lb. beef, thinly sliced
   2 onions, sliced
   1 pack mushrooms, sliced
   1 pack bean sprouts
   1-2 green peppers, sliced
   1 pack tofu, cubed
   1/4-1/2 cabbage, cut coarsely
Dipping Sauce:
   1/2 c. sake (Japanese rice wine) or sherry
   1/3 c. soy sauce (Kikkoman)
   dash monosodium glutamate (optional)
   1 t. mustard or grated fresh ginger
Dip meat and vegetables in sauce and eat with steamed rice.

– Elaine Wright, Okinawa, Japan

Old Indian Stew
Nicaragua

Indio Viejo
(EEN-dee-oh
vee-AY-hoh)

Serves 4-6

Boil until tender:
> 1 lb. stewing beef

When cool, pull into threads with fingers. Save the broth.

Mix with water and broth to make a thick mixture:
> 1 c. corn meal

Set aside.

In a cooking pot, fry together:
> 1 onion, chopped
> 1 tomato, chopped
> 3 cloves garlic, chopped
> 1 green pepper, finely chopped, if desired
> shredded meat

When vegetables are soft, add corn meal mixture and cook, stirring constantly for about 20 minutes or until the consistency is thick and it is brown in color. Add broth as needed during cooking.

Add:
> 2 sprigs mint, chopped
> 1-2 T. lemon juice
> salt to taste

This is a dish eaten in many Nicaraguan homes. The consistency is thick and heavy but the flavor is good and contents nourishing.

– Juana Hernández, Managua, Nicaragua

Friday evening picnic hosted by Beth and Glenn Frey: Menu was refreshing mint lemonade, sloppy Joes, baked beans (substitute raw peanuts pre-cooked), homemade ice cream, and some fresh fruit in season (papaya, mangos, oranges or guavas).

– Miriam Wenger

Meat and Macaroni
Egypt

Macarona bel Bishemal
(Mak-a-ROW-nah bell-bish-eh-MALL)

Boil **1 lb. macaroni** (preferably the 1 1/2 in. long hollow tube kind), then strain.
Fry: **1 large onion, diced.**
Add and cook until brown:
 2 lb. ground beef
Add:
 pinch of salt and pepper.
Make bishemal:
 On low heat, melt **2 T. butter.**
Add and cook until yellow:
 3 T. flour
Add, a little at a time, and stir constantly until thick:
 3 (or more) c. chicken soup
 1 c. milk
Mix the macaroni, meat, and half of the bishemal; pour into a baking pan. Cover the mixture with the remainder of the bishemal and top with **2 beaten eggs**. Bake at 350° for 45 minutes or until brown.

 – Brian and Marcelle Zook, Egypt

I n Zimbabwe, as is the case in many African countries, sharing food and drink is part of hospitality. Individuals and whole family units are weighed and assessed as to how generous they are according to how readily they share their homes and food.

 – Doris Dube, Bulawayo, Zimbabwe

Zimbabwean Stew
Zimbabwe

Serves 4

Fry lightly until browned:
1 lb. beef, cubed
Add and sauté lightly:
2 T. oil
2 small onions, chopped
Add and cook:
3 ripe medium-size tomatoes, chopped
salt and pepper to taste
Add:
1¹/₂ c. water
Simmer until meat is tender.
Serve with rice or corn meal poridge.

Vegetables such as carrots, green beans, peas, or potatoes may be added after the addition of liquid. Sometimes green leafy vegetables, e.g., cabbage or spinach, are added before the addition of water and fried a little. In that case water is reduced to less than ¹/₂ cup. Every Zimbabwean girl, as young as the age of 10 years, is able to make this stew. A variation of this recipe is eaten nearly every day.

– Jeste Mlilo, Bulawayo, Zimbabwe

The Zambians and Zimbabweans are marvelous hosts and hostesses. They will share their best, even if it hurts to share.

– Ardys E. Thuma, Bradford, OH
(Zambia and Zimbabwe)

Curried Meat
Zambia

Serves 4-6

Fry or cook:
 1/2 lb. beef or lamb, cubed
Heat 2 T. oil or drippings and sauté:
 1 large onion, sliced
Add and heat until it bubbles:
 1 t. curry powder
Then add:
 2-3 peeled tomatoes, chopped
 2 t. chutney
 a few raisins
 1 t. salt
 1 t. lemon juice
 1 c. water
Stir the prepared meat into the curry sauce. Cook slowly with lid on saucepan for about 1 hour or less. Serve on boiled rice.

Sambals are small dishes of:
chopped tomatoes, chopped onions, sliced bananas, chutney or apricot jam, raisins, peanuts, shredded coconut, pineapple chunks.

Serve the curried meat in gravy on steamed rice. Then the sambals are placed on top of the meat and gravy.

Anna says, "This is more than a delicious dish - it's an experience!"

– Anna Graybill, Hershey, PA (Zambia)

Cornbread Taco Bake
Southern USA

Serves 6

In skillet brown and drain:
  1½ lb. ground beef
Add:
  1 package (1⅛ oz.) Durkee taco seasoning
  ½ c. water
  12 oz. whole kernel corn (drained)
  ½ c. green peppers, chopped
  8 oz. tomato sauce
Pour into two-quart casserole.
In a bowl prepare according to directions:
  8½ oz. package corn muffin mix
Add:
  ½-2.8 oz. can Durkee French fried onions
Spoon muffin mix around outer edge of dish.
Bake uncovered at 400° for 20 minutes.
Top with:
  ⅓ c. shredded cheddar cheese and
  remaining canned onions.
Bake two to three minutes longer.

– Avelene Weber, West Milton, OH

Zimbabwean women cooking rice

Meat-Stuffed Grape Leaves *Jordan*

Serves 4-8

In the Middle East, a host will spend beyond his means or kill the last chicken in the village to entertain guests. As soon as you empty your plate, the host fills it again — the guest has no choice. If you do not want more food you must not empty your plate.

Combine for stuffing:
  1¹/₂ lb. ground lamb or beef or a mixture of both (should have some fat)
  1 c. onions, chopped
  1 c. canned tomatoes
  ³/₄ c. raw rice
  ¹/₂ c. fresh parsley, chopped or ¹/₄ c. dry parsley flakes
  salt and pepper to taste
Prepare:
  1 8-oz. jar of grape leaves
  2 c. canned tomatoes
  ¹/₂ c. water
  ¹/₂ t. salt

Before stuffing the leaves, line a heavy pot with a layer of leaves or use a trivet to prevent the bottom layer from sticking to the pot. Separate and drape some of the leaves around the inside of the pot. Now shape a portion of stuffing into a small cylinder and place it on a leaf near the stem end, after pinching off the remaining piece of stem. Fold down the lobes near the stem, fold in the sides, and roll toward the point of the leaf. Arrange the stuffed leaves side by side in the pot, making as many layers as necessary. Pour the canned tomatoes over the stuffed leaves, add salt and water. Cover, bring to a boil, lower heat, and simmer about one hour. Test for doneness by tasting one (or more!). Serve hot.

Serves 4-8 depending on whether the stuffed leaves are the whole meal or a side dish. Add a salad, bread or rolls and you have a meal. Leftovers may be frozen.

Option 1: Substitute: ¹/₄ c. coarse ground bulgur for the same amount of rice, or ¹/₄ c. wheat germ for part of the rice.

Option 2: Top with plain yogurt – a delicious combination.

*– Ethel Kreider,
Lancaster, PA (Jordan)*

93

Chicken Curry
India

(mur-gee tahr-KAHR-ee)

Serves 10

In 2 T. hot oil, toast:
  1/4 t. cumin seeds
  2 black cardamom pods
  1 white cardamom pod
When oil crackles, add and fry until brown:
  3 large onions, chopped
  1 1-inch piece of ginger root, sliced
    or 1/2 t. ginger powder
  6 cloves garlic, sliced
Mix the following with 2 T. water and fry with onion mixture for 2 minutes:
  1/2 t. ground cumin
  3 T. ground coriander
  1/4 t. turmeric
  1/4 t. cinnamon
  1/8 t. cloves
  1/4 t. salt or to taste
  1/4 t. hot red chili powder or to taste
Add 2-lb. fryer chicken, cut in 1-inch pieces, including bones.
Brown chicken in above curry mixture.
Add 1 c. water now, add more as water is absorbed.
Cover and cook slowly for 30 minutes, allowing flavors to blend.
Toward end of cooking time add:
  1 large tomato, chopped
Allow to steam for 5 minutes. More water may be added for a gravy consistency.

Options: May serve with brown or white rice. Also lentils can be served as an accompaniment. This chicken curry is "mouth watering" good when served on a bed of fluffy, white rice. We often ate chicken curry and rice with our fingers, served on a banana leaf in the courtyard or on a veranda.

– *Beulah Arnold, Campbellsville, KY (India)*
– *Gulabi McCarty, Ridgeway, ON (India)*

I n Zambia when you arrive at a village, someone will start running to catch a chicken. Then you know you have a nice long visit ahead of you while the chicken is caught, cleaned, cooked and, finally, served. This is how I learned to cook Zambian style as I squatted around the cooking fire with the women of the village.

– Ardys E. Thuma, Bradford, OH (Zambia and Zimbabwe)

Chicken Pie Québec

Paté au Poulet
(Pah-tay oh poo-lay)

Serves 6

Melt in large saucepan:
   1/2 c. margarine
Add:
   1/2 c. flour
Slowly and stirring constantly add:
   3 c. chicken broth
   Salt and pepper to taste
Heat on medium heat until it bubbles one minute. Remove from heat.
Add:
   3 c. chicken or turkey, cooked and cubed
   1 1/2 c. carrots, cooked and sliced
   1 c. peas, cooked (optional)
Pour into 13 x 9-inch pan.
Cover with pastry crust.
Bake at 425° for 20 minutes or until golden.

This is good served as a hot lunch or an evening meal.

– Yolande Shink, Romuald, Québec

L eora Yoder remembers celebrating Christmas with fellow missionaries who feasted on American turkey shipped in glass jars by a Pennsylvania pastor who, with his wife, made it a practice for many years to provide a "homestyle" dinner for the missionaries.

Charcoal Broiled Chicken on a Skewer
Japan

Yakitori
(Yah-kee-TOE-ree)

Cut in 1-in. pieces and place on bamboo skewers:
   2 chicken breasts
Prepare basting sauce by simmering for 15 minutes:
   ³/₄ c. sake (Japanese rice wine) or sherry
   ³/₄ c. soy sauce (Kikkoman)
   ¹/₄ c. sugar
   ¹/₂ t. grated fresh ginger (optional)
Brush sauce over chicken skewers and broil over charcoal. Turn frequently, brushing more sauce over meat. Serve hot. Chicken livers are also delicious cooked in this sauce.

– Elaine Wright, Okinawa, Japan

In many Indian and Nepali homes, the main meal consists of rice or chappatis served with lentils or a vegetable curry. On the way home from work, a member of the family may stop at the vegetable market to purchase a fresh, seasonal vegetable and a few onions for the evening curry dish. Occasionally, in non-vegetarian homes, chicken or goat meat will provide the basis for the curry. In rural areas (India is still mainly rural) the vegetables come from the twice-weekly market held in a central location.

Chicken Tikka
India

(Moor-gee tee-kah)

Serves 8

Blend the following ingredients in blender:
$1/4$ c. lemon juice
2 T. vinegar
$1/4$ c. parsley
2 cloves garlic
$1/2$ t. ground ginger
$1 1/2$ t. paprika
$1/2$ t. cayenne pepper
1 t. turmeric
1 t. ground cumin
1 t. salt (or to taste)
$1/2$ c. plain nonfat yogurt or tomato juice
Pour sauce over, refrigerate and marinate for 2 hours:
2 lbs. boneless, skinless chicken breast cut into small pieces
Add:
$1/2$ c. frozen peas
3 medium potatoes, cubed
Cook slowly for 45 minutes to 1 hour. Add water as the chicken cooks, 1-2 T. at a time, to create the curry sauce.
Serve with steamed rice.
Method of serving: first pass the platter of steamed rice. Then pass this curry and place on the top or to the side of the rice. Best served with lentils and a chutney of sliced onions and tomatoes.

This is one of several meat or vegetable curries I make when our children come home for a meal. They know that they can expect Indian food which became a family favorite while they were growing up in India. Now our children's spouses enjoy it with us and the grandchildren love it as hot, if not hotter, than the rest of us. This ethnic food brings back wonderful memories of delicious meals we were served in Indian homes over a span of 12 years.

– *Erma J. Sider, Mechanicsburg, PA (Bihar, India)*

Chicken Biriani
India

Murghi Biriani
(Mur-gee beer-ee-
YAN-ee)

Serves 8

Part A
Cut up in small pieces:
   3 lb. chicken
Add to chicken and marinate for 30 minutes:
   1 c. plain yogurt
   ¹/₂ c. onion, chopped
   2 T. coriander powder
   ¹/₂ t. fresh ginger root, grated
   1 t. garlic, minced
   1 t. turmeric
   ¹/₄ t. black pepper

Part B
Sauté together until onion turns light brown:
   ¹/₄ c. butter, melted
   ¹/₄ c. vegetable oil
   1 med. onion, finely chopped
   2 cloves garlic, minced
   8 whole cloves
   8 whole cardamom
   1 t. salt
   1 c. water

After Part B is sautéed, add Part A and sauté further, stirring frequently. When chicken has changed color and sauce seems dry, add 1 cup water, lower heat and simmer for 30 minutes. Add a chicken bouillon cube to enough additional water to make 4 cups curry sauce. Remove chicken pieces from sauce and set aside. Heat this curry sauce until almost boiling.

Part C
Rinse and soak for 30-40 minutes:
   3 c. Basmati rice or long grain rice
Sauté in a sauce pan until onion is wilted:
   1 small onion, sliced thin
   4 oz. butter or oil
   1 clove garlic, minced

(continued on next page)

(continued from previous page)

Chicken Biriani

4 whole cloves
8 cardamom, gently crushed
2-two inch sticks cinnamon
Transfer rice and this mixture to an 8 x 13 inch
baking dish and stir until rice is warmed through.
Add the boiling curry sauce (Part B) and stir.
Cover and bake at 325° for 30 minutes. Place the
chicken pieces in the rice, cover again and bake
for another 30 minutes.
Serve with chutney and raita salad.

– A. J. Mann, Elizabethtown, PA (Bihar, India)

**Chicken in
Coconut Milk
Thailand**

Cook 6 chicken drumsticks until tender, in this
broth:
2 c. water
milk drained from 1 fresh coconut*
$1/2$ c. thin slices of galangal
1 stem lemon grass, sliced into thin rings
and crushed
3 T. fish sauce
Season at end of cooking with:
juice of 3 lemons
3-4 kaffir lime leaves
10 hot chilies, crushed
Put into serving dish and sprinkle with coriander
leaves, chopped.
*May substitute for fresh coconut milk by mixing
2 c. water with $1/2$ lb. grated coconut and then
squeezing out milk.

– Kathy Brubaker, Bangkok, Thailand

Chicken and Vegetables Cooked in Broth
Japan

Mizutaki
(Mee-zoo-TAH-kee)

Serves 4

Cook in 5 c. water for 30 minutes:
4 chicken thighs or breasts
Season to taste. Cut up chicken.
At the table use an electric fry pan. Add:
**chicken
4 c. of broth
4 long onions or leeks, cut diagonally
8 oz. package mushrooms, shiitake or enoki
8 oz. package tofu, cubed
1 Chinese cabbage, cut coarsely**
Cook until cabbage is tender.
In each person's soup bowl add **soy sauce** and **lemon juice** to taste (monosodium glutonate optional). Add broth, vegetables, and chicken from frying pan. Eat with rice, in separate bowl, using chopsticks or pour over bowl of rice and eat with spoon, like thick soup. Especially good served in winter.

– Ruth Zook, Mechanicsburg, PA (Japan)

Takanobu Tojo and I had become good friends after he had shared some significant theological insights with me ten years earlier. When the group picture was taken at the first International Brethren in Christ Fellowship meeting at Grantham, in 1978, we were side by side.

But this time, in 1981, Tojo and his bride of a few months, entertained Velma and me in their home overnight. Next morning, Tojo led us through the intricacies and beauty of a "tea ceremony." This pastor/teacher was careful, as a true friend, to help us at one of our points of real need–we know so very little about the importance of going "very slow."

Tojo, the eminent scholar/theologian, is first and foremost a true Christian brother.

*– J. Wilmer Heisey,
Mount Joy, PA*

Tonga Chicken *Zambia*

Nkuku
(In-koo-koo)

Serves 5

Brown in 2 T. oil:
  1 chicken, cut in pieces
Add and cook on medium heat for 30 minutes:
  4 medium tomatoes, chopped
  1 small onion, diced
Mix together:
  1 t. curry powder
  1 T. flour
  1¹/₂ c. water
  1 t. salt
Add to chicken mixture and cook until thickened.
Serve with nshima (cornmeal porridge).

This is a typical dish served when visitors come to a village.

– Shelly Muleya, Mizinga Village, Choma, Zambia
– Arbys E. Thuma, Bradford, OH (Zambia)

Tonga Chicken

When we lived in Zambia, the first night our sons arrived home from school and the hostel in Bulawayo, Zimbabwe, we would have Tonga Chicken. Meryl, our eldest, especially enjoyed it and always asked for Tonga Chicken sometime during the holidays. Since the girls who helped me in the kitchen knew how to prepare it so well, and I often made the day's trip to Choma and back to get Phil and Meryl at the train station, they could prepare this with no help from me. As we drove into the driveway, Meryl and Phil could see the two black pots on little fires outside our kitchen door. At once they knew we were having Tonga Chicken for dinner. With some of their favorite desserts made by me the day before, it was a joyous homecoming for them and for us.

– Ardys. E. Thuma,
Bradford, OH (Zimbabwe)

Chicken Stew
Cuba

Fricasé De Pollo
(Free-kah-SAY day POH-yoh)

Serves 6-8

In a large pot sauté in $1/4$ c. olive oil:
1 whole chicken, skinned and cut up
1 large onion, cubed
1 green pepper, cubed
2-3 garlic cloves, mashed
Add:
2 bouillon cubes
1 t. cumin
$1/2$ t. salt
dash pepper
After browning add and stir:
4 oz. can tomato sauce
1 t. turmeric or saffron
3-4 potatoes, cut in chunks
3-4 carrots, cut in chunks
salt, if needed
water, to cover chicken
Simmer about 1 hour.

Serve over rice. Goes nicely with a garden salad. Leftovers make great chicken soup by using the deboned chicken, and adding water and noodles.

My grandmother taught me this very typical Cuban dish when I asked her to teach me how to cook. We measured nothing and tasted everything. I am guessing at the measurements since I do not use any special measuring devices. Therefore, feel free to add or take away according to your tastes. Throughout the island there are many varieties of this particular dish.

Excellent for any occasion.

– Merly Bundy, Madrid, Spain

At Cuatro Caminos, Cuba, the people had to use food ration stamps. But that did not prevent them from putting on a real spread. Returning from the church, there was a convergence on Juana Garcia's house – people and delicacies began to appear. The connoisseurs of good food had grown most of their own garden food, and kept rabbits in their back yards.

We sat down to a table full of good dishes – rice, wonderful beans, fried banana chips, tasty rabbit, and many more dishes. Through sharing, and mastery of the culinary arts, all that goes with good food and fellowship was in lavish abundance in Cuba on that Sunday afternoon, where brothers and sisters in Christ enjoyed one another's fellowship.

– J. Wilmer Heisey,
Mount Joy, PA

Chicken Enchilada *Navajo*

Serves 6

Cook and removed from bones:
    2 lb. chicken pieces
Mix together:
    1 can cream of mushroom soup
    1 medium can enchilada sauce
Layer, in a 2-quart casserole, half of each:
    chicken
    6 corn tortillas, large
    soup mixture
Repeat the above layers. Top with:
    1 lb. cheddar cheese, grated
Bake at 350° for 50 minutes

– Ethel Bundy, Mechanicsburg, PA (New Mexico)

Chicken with Vegetables and Tofu
China

Serves 4

Cut into ¹/₂-inch cubes and return to refrigerator:
  10 oz. firm tofu, drained
Cut into thin strips:
  1 chicken breast, skinned and boned
Marinate chicken for at least 10 minutes in:
  1 T. cornstarch
  1 T. soy sauce
  1 clove garlic, minced
Blend:
  ³/₄ c. chicken broth
  1 t. vinegar
  1 T. cornstarch
  2 T. soy sauce
In very hot wok or skillet heat:
  1 T. oil
Add chicken, stir-fry 2 minutes, remove from wok.
In same wok, heat:
  2 T. oil
Add and stir-fry 2 minutes:
  1 medium zucchini, julienned
  1 red or green bell pepper, cut into strips
  ¹/₄ lb. mushrooms, quartered
  1 t. fresh ginger root, minced
  4 green onions, cut into 2-inch lengths
    (whites only)
Add and stir-fry 1 minute:
  green onion tops
Add chicken and broth mixture and stir until thickened.
Fold in tofu and heat through.

Serve at noon or for the evening meal, either with rice or noodles.

Tofu is soybean curd and is a good source of vegetable protein. Oriental people often use it as a meat substitute. Tofu by itself is bland and tasteless, but added to dishes with broth, it takes on that flavor. It's tasty in a beef or chicken soup. My international guests enjoy this dish.

– Mim Stern, Philadelphia, PA

One of the difficulties in learning the Chinese language is that Chinese is a tonal language: the same syllable can be pronounced with different tones for four different meanings. Take, for example, the syllable "ji" (pronounced "jee"). If this syllable is pronounced using a high, flat tone, it means "chicken." If it is pronounced in a rising tone as if asking a question ("Jee?"), it can mean "illness." If it is pronounced in a tone that falls from a high pitch to a low pitch, it can be a person's surname.

When my teammate and I were introduced to a young man named Mr. Ji, we remembered the syllable correctly but failed to get the right tone. You can imagine our embarrassment when, after some months of acquaintance with him, his girlfriend gently informed us that all this time we had been calling him "Mr. Chicken!"

– *Joyce Peterman,*
Manheim, PA

We touch our visitor's souls by creating a comfortable atmosphere, listening carefully to their words and hearts, offering kindness and encouragement . . . anything that fills inner needs and renews spirits. In turn, we can humbly allow guests to nurture and spiritually refuel us. Caring for the soul constitutes a give-and-take relationship.

– *Discipleship Journal, Judith Couchman, Issue 98, 1997*

Stir-Fry Chicken and Vegetables
Japan

Cut into bite–size pieces:
  2 chicken breasts
Marinate in:
  $^1/_4$ c. soy sauce
  2 T. mirin (sweetened rice wine or
    cooking sherry)
Fry chicken until just done; do not overcook.
Add and cook until thickened:
  1 c. bouillon
  2 T. cornstarch
In separate fry pan, stir-fry vegetables in oil until
crisp-tender:
  1 onion
  8 oz. bean sprouts
  8 oz. shiitake mushrooms
  6 oz. broccoli or sugar peas, or any
    seasonal vegetable
Add vegetables to meat mixture. Heat through
and serve over rice or noodles (drained ramen
noodles make a quick meal).

– Ruth Zook, Mechanicsburg, PA (Japan)

I planned to visit our son, John, when he was teaching at Choma Secondary School in Zambia. While there I wanted to have a party for many of our friends. Could I carry a turkey all the way to Zambia? Into my carry-on bag went the frozen turkey, packed in dry ice! In London airport came the only question about it on my trip. When the bag went through the scanner, the handsome young fellow asked, "Is it a turkey?" When I agreed, he replied, "I've seen worse!"

One week later 14 of us enjoyed the turkey. Since John's oven door didn't close properly I took it to a neighbor's oven which cooked it faster than I expected, so that the popper popped four hours ahead of time. Another problem arose when the electricity outage came just at the time to cook the potatoes. But the dinner planned for six o'clock came off at seven-thirty with lots of good fellowship!

– Mary Long,
Grantham, PA

Filipino Chicken
Philippines

Serves 4-6

In large skillet place:
1 frying chicken cut in pieces (or two breasts
cut in half)
Spoon over the chicken:
4 T. vinegar
Salt and pepper to taste
Crush and place among chicken pieces:
3-4 cloves garlic
Add and simmer until tender:
2 c. water
Spoon over all:
2 T. soy sauce
Sprinkle over top:
1 t. oregano
Cook until most of the liquid is absorbed and
chicken is browned. Cooking time: 30-40 min.

Delicious served with steamed rice. This comes
from my husband's voluntary service days in the
Philippines. When I prepare this, he says it brings
back the sights, sounds, and smells of Filipino
villages.

– Marilyn Smith, Souderton, Pennsylvania

I tell you, though he will not get up and give him the bread
because he is his friend, yet because of the man's boldness
he will get up and give him as much as he needs.

– Luke 11:8

Tandoori Chicken
India

(Ton-DOOR-ee
MUR-gee)

Serves 6

Place in 9x13-inch lightly greased baking pan:
   12 pieces of chicken
Blend (in blender):
   2 large onions, sliced
   2 cloves garlic
   3 T. oil
   1 cup yogurt
   2 T. lemon juice
   1 t. salt
   1 T. ground coriander
   1 T. ground cumin
   $^1/_2$ t. ground ginger
   1 t. turmeric
   $^1/_2$ t. cinnamon
   $^1/_4$ t. cayenne pepper
   $^1/_4$ t. black pepper
   1 T. curry powder
Pour over chicken and marinate four hours in refrigerator. Bake at 375° for 50 minutes.

Serve with fluffy rice and vegetables.
Option: **Tomato juice** can be substituted for yogurt. Quartered **potatoes** mixed in with chicken make a nice addition.

– *A. J. Mann, Elizabethtown, PA (Bihar, India)*
– *Erma Sider, Mechanicsburg, PA (Bihar, India)*

Thank you, God, for these hands. They will work. The left one for myself and the right one for you.

– *Rhoda, Zambia*

We had hoped to return from a Sunday service at a camp to the west of the Navajo Mission before the frost was out of the ground. But, as the service had lasted longer than expected, we had no more than started home when we were stuck in the mud. For the next more than three hours Elinor (Nicholson) and I pulled sagebrush while Lynn jacked up the wheels so we could put it under them, and shoveled sand. Going only a few car lengths between moves, we were finally almost at the top of a long hill when the clutch burned out.

We were still miles from home and it was dark, but we started walking toward home, Brother Nicholson carrying Lynn Stephen on his back. Several hours later, we had arrived at Antonio Begay's camp, still two and one half miles from home.

Although it was 9:15 in the evening, Lula cordially invited us into their hogan and gave us bread and coffee. Then they gave us their best bed, a mattress on the ground. They gave us extra covers and we never slept better.

In the morning Lula again gave us Navajo bread and coffee, and we walked home. All three of us had blisters on our feet and it was almost two weeks before we finally got the car back home.

Antonio Begay, a medicine man, and his gracious wife, Lula, remained some of our very best neighbors until their deaths. Both of them are buried in the Mission cemetery.

– Written by J. Wilmer Heisey, Mount Joy, PA,
as told by Rosa Eyster

Maria makes tortillas and Tinfón eats them.

– Spanish proverb

Mutton Stew
Navajo
(New Mexico)

'Atsi' Hahaázh
Beezh
(AT-see ha-
HAAZH bayzh)

Serves 8

Combine in a large soup pot the following:
> 2 lb. mutton neck (lamb shoulder roast is
>   very good)
> 2 qt. water
> 2 t. salt
> 1 t. pepper

Cook till tender (1 hr. for shoulder roast, 2-3 for mutton neck). Remove bones. Cool to harden fat and discard. Return the meat and broth to the pot and add:
> 2 large onions, chopped
> 6 large potatoes, diced
> Cabbage, squash, carrots or other
>   vegetables may be added if available

Simmer until tender (about 20 min.) Serve with Fry Bread.

'Atsi' Hahaázh Beezh is one of four names for mutton stew. The name indicates the amount of meat.

Mutton stew and fry bread are traditional Navajo dishes and are served at all special occasions.

> *– Ernestine Chavez, Annabelle Yazzie,*
> *Rebecca Eldridge, Karen Redfearn,*
> *Bloomfield, NM*

Gideon went in, prepared a young goat, and from an ephah of flour he made bread without yeast. Putting the meat in a basket and its broth in a pot, he brought them out and offered them to him under the oak.

– Judges 6:19

Lamb Curry with Sweet Onions
India

Kheema do Pyaza
(KHEE-mah doh pee-AH-zah)

Serves 6

Heat 2 T. oil in a large, non-stick skillet. When very hot, add and sauté until golden brown:
  2 very large onions, thinly sliced
Remove onions from skillet and set aside.
Add 1 T. oil to same skillet and sauté until soft:
  1 large green pepper, thinly sliced
Remove pepper from skillet and set aside.
In same skillet add and sauté for 30 seconds:
  2 cloves garlic, minced
  1 T. fresh ginger, minced
  1 Jalapeno pepper, minced
Add and sauté, stirring to blend spices with meat:
  2 lb. lean lamb cut in julienne strips
  1 t. ground cumin
  1 t. turmeric
  1 t. cinnamon
  $^1/_4$ t. ground cardamom
  $^1/_2$ t. fennel seeds
  $^1/_2$ t. dried hot red pepper (cayenne)
  salt to taste.
Cook over high heat until the lamb is done (5-7 minutes).
Arrange the lamb on a serving platter. Return the onions and green pepper to the skillet to heat through and spoon the mixture over the lamb.

Serve with hot, fluffy rice.

– A. J. Mann, Elizabethtown, PA (Bihar, India)

Liver Sausage
Navajo

Mix together:

    1 whole liver, heart, fat, and lung of a sheep
       or goat, ground

Add:

    2 medium raw potatoes, peeled, and
       chopped
    ¹/₂ onion, chopped
    2 small celery stalks, chopped
    2 t. salt

Mix well. Put in a clean sheep or goat stomach, and tie with string. Place in 2¹/₂ c. water in a pan and cook slowly for one hour.

– Karen Redfearn, New Mexico

Roast Pig Stomach *Pennsylvania Dutch*

Serves 6-8

Combine for stuffing:
   1¹/₂ lb. ground sausage, cooked and drained
   6 medium or 1 qt. potatoes, chopped
   1 small onion, chopped
   2 c. cabbage, shredded (optional)
Add seasonings (if desired) and mix well.
   1-2 t. salt
   ¹/₂ t. pepper
   1 t. parsley, dried
Fill with stuffing and sew shut:
   1 large pig stomach well-cleaned
Place in roasting pan. Add:
   ¹/₂ c. water
Cover and roast at 350° for 3 hours. Slice and serve with gravy made by adding flour and water to pan drippings, if desired.

Naomi Shenk writes, "Mother would make two or three of these and invite all the family to come home. Some of the 'in-laws' would wrinkle their noses but if they tasted it, they found it was pretty good."

– Naomi A. Shenk, Conestoga, PA
– Arlene Martin, Elizabethtown, PA
– Marian Bomberger, Dillsburg, PA

Martha's problem wasn't cooking, it was the "many things." She was multi-directional, which always makes us oppressed, nervous, burdened, self-pitying, off-balance.

When your eyes are on Him, you begin to develop a reflex action inside you—it may take time—that shuns what's complicating, what's overwhelming. You'll find you want to do less (but do the most important things) to become more.

Fix your eyes on Jesus! Like Mary, focus; that's what I had to learn. Become a "one-thing" person (Luke 10:42).

– Ann Ortlund,
My Sacrifice, His Fire. Word
Publishing, 1993, p.32.

Toad-in-the-Hole
England

Serves 6

Prepare Yorkshire pudding batter (page 144)
Heat **1 T. oil** in baking pan. Pour Yorkshire
pudding into hot oil.
Scatter over top:
    **1 T. chopped onion, fried or steamed
    (optional)**
    **12-16 oz. package sausages
    (can use cubed steak, any meat scraps
    or fresh sausage)**
Bake at 400° for 20-30 minutes until pudding is
well-risen and browned.

– Judy Smith, London, England

This is an 18th century recipe idea when pieces
of meat were baked in batter, giving the dish its
name of Toad-in-the-Hole. It's usually made with
sausages today.

Chinese Cabbage and Pork
Japan

Soak in warm water until soft, and squeeze out
gently:
    1 pack kikurage (Chinese tree ears)
Fry until done:
    1 lb. pork, sliced
Add and stir fry until barely limp:
    2-3 T. soy sauce
    **1 bunch long negi (onions), cut on
    diagonal**
    1 pack kikurage
    Chinese cabbage leaves, cut up
Add if desired:
    monosodium glutamate
Thicken with:
    **2 T. cornstarch in about 1 c. water
    (depending on desired thickening)**
Serve hot with rice.

– Ruth Zook, Mechanicsburg, PA (Japan)

Quick Sweet and Sour Pork
Japan

Marinate for 30 minutes:
> 1 lb. thinly sliced pork

Mix marinade:
> 1 t. salt
> 1 t. soy sauce
> 1 t. sugar

Fry pork until brown and crisp; set aside.
Cut vegetables into bite-size pieces and stir-fry in oil until crisp-tender:
> 1 onion
> 2 carrots
> 2 green peppers, or 1 pack sugar peas

Add meat and 1 can (16 oz.) pineapple pieces.
Prepare sauce:
> $^3/_4$ c. sugar
> $^1/_3$ c. soy sauce
> $^1/_3$ c. vinegar
> $^1/_2$ c. water
> $^1/_4$ c. pineapple juice
> $^1/_4$ c. cornstarch

Cook over low heat until thickened.
Add sauce to meat and vegetables.
Serve over hot rice.

– Ruth Zook, Mechanicsburg, PA (Japan)

W e were eating a delicious supper at the home of a former student and asked what ingredients were used in making the filling for the delicious boiled dumplings. Our Chinese friend intended to say, "Meat and cabbage," but she got the wrong English word and told us, "Meat and garbage!"

– Joyce Peterman, Manheim, PA

Pork Chops in Tomato Sauce
Honduras

Chuleta en Salsa de Tomate
(chew-LAY-tah en SAL-sa day To-MAH-tay)

Remove fat and rub with salt:
  8 large pork chops
Heat 1 T. oil in frying pan and add:
  pork chops
  1 whole clove garlic, minced
Brown on both sides and remove from heat.
In bottom of greased casserole, place:
  5 tomatoes, peeled and chopped
  ¹/₂ c. olives, sliced
  1 T. flour
  1 t. salt
  pepper
Top with browned pork chops and garlic. Pour over 2 T. of the oil used to brown the chops. Bake at 400° for about 1 hour.
Decorate with parsley.

– Yolanda Calderón de Herrera, Tegucigalpa, Honduras

Ham Loaf
Pennsylvania Dutch

Serves 8

Mix well:
  2 lb. ham, ground
  2 lb. fresh lean pork, ground
  ³/₄ c. crackers (saltines), crushed
  ¹/₄ c. onions, chopped
  3 eggs
  1 c. milk
  1 T. chopped parsley
Shape into 2 loaves and put in 9x5x3-inch pans
Combine for syrup to baste or glaze:
  ¹/₂ c. brown sugar
  ¹/₄ c. cider vinegar
  1 t. dry mustard
Boil 1 minute. Pour over loaves. Bake at 350° for 1¹/₂ hours, basting three times.

– Anna Ruth Ressler, Elizabethtown, PA
Martha Wingert, Franklin County, PA

Relish
Zambia

Cut in pieces and fry in 1 T. Oil:
  2 pounds meat (beef, pork, or chicken)
Add when meat is brown:
  1 medium onion, diced
  1 t. salt
  3 medium tomatoes, diced
Cook until vegetables are soft. Add 2 cups water
and simmer for 30 minutes.

– Mrs. L. Hamaseele, pastor's wife at
Macha Brethren in Christ Church, Choma, Zambia

When someone comes to visit a village, they must be fed. An animal, usually a chicken, is killed. Even if the visitor has been expected, the chicken will not be killed until he or she arrives. All animals are very valuable so to kill an animal for your own family is unthinkable. You greet the people in the village and talk while the food is being prepared. When it is ready you are taken into the house and the food is served to you. Generally the visitors eat alone, and after the meal the host rejoins you. This is done so that you will feel comfortable eating and be able to eat only what you want. Sometimes the host will join you, either sitting with you while you eat or he will eat with you. If your host joins you, it will be the man or men; the women will not join in the eating.

– Ann Marie Parry,
Danville, PA
(Choma, Zambia)

Ham and Potato Casserole
Québec

Casserole au Jambon et aux Pommes de Terre
(Kass-rohl oh Jah-bohn ay oh Pahm de Tayr)

Serves 6

Cook in boiling water for 5 minutes:
2¹/₂ lbs. or 6 c. raw potatoes, sliced
1 c. onions, sliced
2 c. water
1 t. salt
Cook and cube:
2 c. ham
Combine for sauce:
10-oz. can cream of mushroom soup
1 c. milk
1 T. prepared mustard
1 T. parsley, chopped
¹/₄ t. pepper
In 13 x 9-inch greased pan, layer half of potatoes and onions, half of cubed ham, and half of the sauce. Repeat layers. Garnish with buttered bread cubes.
Bake at 375° for 35-40 minutes.

Great for a hot lunch or an evening meal. Quebec families often serve hot full meals at noon, a reminder of their rural roots. Most children walk, or are bused, home from school for this important meal.

– Lucie Boulanger, Romuald, Quebec

The men of Lamao would go into the mountain for wild pig with their dogs, spears and one gun. If successful, there was always celebration and ceremony to go with it. Velma soon learned that when Maggalis came up the steps with that special "satisfied look," we were in for a treat. He handed us a nice portion of fresh meat. Among the Tinguians, you eat meat on special occasions!

– J. Wilmer Heisey,
Mount Joy, PA
(MCC, Philippines)

Wild Boar Stew
Japan

Inoshishi
(Een-oh-SHEE-shee)

Fry in oil:
    3¹/₂ oz. pork per person
Cut into bite-size pieces and add:
    satoimo (taro)
    gobo (burdock)
    kabu (small round turnips)
    long onions or leeks
    carrots
    tofu
    shiitake mushrooms
Add and cook until vegetables are soft:
    2 T. soy sauce
    2 T. sugar
    2 T. sake
    pinch of monosodium glutamate
        (optional) and enough water to
        make broth
Add:
    ¹/₂ c. miso (crushed soy beans) mixed with
    ¹/₃ c. milk
Heat through but do not boil the miso. Serve
with rice.

We were served this delicious stew in the mountains of Yamaguchi Ken. It can also be made with rabbit but I usually use the readily available thinly sliced pork. Start with about 3¹/₂ oz. pork per person and include a variety of vegetables.

– Ruth Zook, Mechanicsburg, PA (Japan)

Whether a child or an old man, or a youth come to thy house, he is to be treated with respect, for of all men, thy guest is thy superior.
– Sanskrit proverb

Shepherd's Pie
England

Serves 6

Scrub, cook and peel:

2 lb. potatoes

Slice thin two of the potatoes and set aside. Mash the rest, season with salt and pepper to taste, and mix with:

1 c. milk
2 T. butter
meat mixture

In 2 T. oil sauté:

1 c. onion, chopped
1 lb. meat (beef, lamb, or mixed veal and pork), ground
3 cloves garlic, cut fine

Drain excess fat.

Add part of:

1 c. broth

Sprinkle 1 T. flour or corn starch on top, slowly add remaining broth and simmer to a rich sauce adding the following flavorings to taste:

1 T. tomato concentrate or paste (optional)
1 T. Worcestershire sauce or 1$^1/_2$ t. wine vinegar
$^1/_4$ t. thyme
$^1/_2$ t. salt
$^1/_4$ t. black pepper
Cayenne pepper (optional)

Pour into a 10-inch round baking dish. Spread mashed potatoes on top and, with the slices, make a ring around the edge. Sprinkle with 2 T. **Parmesan cheese or grated cheddar.** Heat at 375° for about 20-30 minutes. Increase heat a few minutes to brown cheese.

Options: I often add frozen peas or carrots to the meat mixture to stretch it!

– Judy Smith, London, England

When a couple gets married, the boy's family is responsible for the wedding arrangements and the food, in addition to the Labola or bride price. The wedding is held at the boy's village and often the girl's parents do not attend. The family of the groom will send the hind leg of an animal (cow) to the parents of the bride if they do not come, so they can have a part of the celebration.

When a couple decides to get married, the families decide on a Labola. Among other things, this includes animals, mainly cows. The average price in the Macha area is four cows, although this varies with the education of the girl. The son of a friend is getting married soon and the bride price includes four cows and three pigs.

– Ann Marie Parry,
Danville, PA
(Choma, Zambia)

Boiled Potatoes and Meat
Japan

Niku Jaga
(Nee-koo JAH-gah)

Serves 6

Slice into thin strips and saute in 1 T. oil until browned:
 ¹/₂ lb. beef or pork
Add and sauté a little more:
 10 small potatoes, peeled and quartered
 1 small onion, thinly sliced
Add and boil gently, skimming off foam, if it forms, until potatoes are done (most of liquid should be gone):
 2 c. water
 1 T. sugar
 2 T. Japanese soy sauce
 1 t. Hondashi (optional)
 3 T. Sake (Japanese rice wine, optional
 1 T. Mirin (Japanese sweet wine, optional)

This dish is tastier if you prepare it in the morning, allow it to cool to room temperature and then reheat for a quick evening meal. Serve with rice and a salad.

– Dora Kawate, Dillsburg, PA (Tokyo, Japan)

T he fourth International Brethren in Christ Fellowship convened in Purnea, Bihar, India. Now it was over. The last goat curry dinner was finished, handshakes, salaams and "God be with you" benedictions were given. Then 41 internationals, complete with multiple suitcases and flight bags, rushed to find a seat in the private coach of our Calcutta-bound train. We had everything we needed: purified water for all, bedding supplied with the coach, enough berths to go around. But what would we do for food on this long, overnight trip?

Well, very soon along came Trudy and Jack McClane, and Bill Hoke with their big bag of food for all. For each

Japanese Meatballs
Japan

Niku Dango
(Nee-koo DAN-goh)

Serves 6

Mix:
- 1 lb. ground meat (beef or mix of beef and pork)
- 1 onion, finely minced
- 2 T. Japanese soy sauce
- 1 T. sugar
- 1 t. salt
- 2 T. cornstarch
- 2 T. ginger root, finely minced

Form meat mixture into 1-inch balls
In frying pan, brown quickly on all sides with a little oil.
Boil the following, then drop meatballs into sauce:
- 1¹/₂ c. water
- 1 T. sugar
- 2 T. soy sauce

Boil meat balls 10 minutes.
Thicken with 1 T. cornstarch dissolved in ¹/₄ c. cold water.

Tasty with hot rice and a green or yellow vegetable. It's easier to make nicely shaped meat balls if your hands are wet.

– Dora Kawate, Dillsburg, PA (Tokyo, Japan)

(continued from previous page)
compartment (4–6 people) there was a loaf of fresh white bread, a jar of jam, cookies, bananas and oranges. "Oh, sorry folks, no utensils for spreading the jam and no peanut butter either." Some travellers came prepared for every emergency so soon a spoon or two was located in our luggage.

Manna from heaven it may not have been, but surely the shared experience of eating sticky jam sandwiches on an Indian train with folk from Mexico, Honduras, Venezuela, Nicaragua, Zambia, Zimbabwe, Malawi, the USA and Canada was a glimmer of our future fellowship "when we all get to heaven."

– Erma J. Sider, Mechanicsburg, PA (Bihar, India)

Country Loaf
Québec

**Pain de
Compagne**
(Pan dew cam-pan-
yeh)

Makes 35 slices

Cover bottom of loaf pan (9x5x3) with half of:
 1/2 lb. uncooked bacon.
Mix together:
 1 1/2 lb. ground pork
 1 1/2 lb. ground veal
 1 c. fine bread crumbs
 2 cloves garlic, minced
 1/4 c. onion, finely chopped
 1/2 c. parsely, chopped
 2 eggs, lightly beaten
 1 t. thyme
 2 t. salt
 1/2 t. pepper
Press lightly in bacon-layered pan. Cover with rest
of bacon
Bake at 375° for 1 1/2-2 hours.
Cool and remove from pan. Refrigerate and slice
cold. The flavor improves if made in advance.
Serve in slices with soft or toasted bread (long
thin French bread is preferred).
Freezes well.

This might be part of a buffet menu, a lunch
served with soup, or a late night snack with
friends.

In the space of two generations Québec went
from one of the highest birthrates in the world to
one of the lowest. Large rural families living
through long, cold winters needed hearty meals.
Meat slices or spreads added to bread helped
stretch the main course of cooked ham or
chicken, potatoes and carrots. Now this might be
served to stretch a meal when all those married
children have their family get-togethers!

Option: Use bacon as topping only.

– Therese Baillargeon, Maurice, Québec

Multi-Meat Pie Québec

Cipaille
(See-pie-yeh)

Cover bottom and sides of a casserole with pie crust.

Mix the following ingredients, place in pie crust, and cover with top pie crust:

- ³/₄ lb. pork, cubed (uncooked)
- ¹/₂ lb. veal, cubed (uncooked)
- ¹/₂ lb. beef, cubed (uncooked)
- ³/₄ lb. cooked chicken, cubed (or turkey or caribou)
- 5 potatoes, cubed (uncooked)
- 1 large onion, chopped
- 1 t. chicken bouillon concentrate (powder and/or liquid)
- 1 t. beef bouillon concentrate
- 1 T. parsley
- 1-2 cloves garlic, minced
- 1 t. salt (or to taste)
- ¹/₂ t. pepper (or to taste)
- 1¹/₂ c. carrots, sliced (optional)

Bake at 250° for 6 hours. Serve as an evening meal. Flavor is enhanced if prepared in advance and served, after reheating, the next day.
Serve as an evening meal.

This is a good substantial meal for a winter evening. When doubled it provides for that special family gathering. In earlier days, the Québecois used meat, potatoes, and carrots as the main elements of their diet, reflecting the harsh winter climate and short growing season.

– Sylvie St-Hilaire, Beauport, Québec

Esau . . . prepared some tasty food and brought it to his father. Then he said to him, "My father, sit up and eat some of my game, so that you may give me your blessing."

– Gensis 27:31

Meat Pie
Québec

Pâté a la Viande
(Pay-tay ah lah
vee-ahnd)

Makes 4-5
9-inch pies

Pastry for four to five 2-crust 9-inch pies
Mix:
> **3 lb. ground pork or 1¹/₂ lb. each of
> ground pork and ground beef or veal
> 1 large Spanish onion, chopped
> 1 t. salt
> 1 large garlic clove, minced
> 1 t. savoury
> ¹/₂ t. ground cloves**

Put into a medium-size kettle. Add water until meat is barely covered and simmer two hours (most of the water should cook away).
Add to meat mixture so it holds together:
fresh bread broken into pieces (without crust)
Pour cooked pork mixture into pastry-lined pans and cover with pastry. Bake at 375° until tops are browned. (Milk brushed on top just before baking makes the tops golden.)

Serve as a main dish for an evening meal, hot lunch, or part of a big holiday meal.

Pork was and still is the popular choice of meat in Québec. Meat, whether pork or beef or poultry, is often simmered and made into stews or pies. This meat pie is traditional Québecois holiday fare. It is included in the family "réveillons," the midnight suppers now usually served buffet style, on Christmas Eve and New Year's Eve. The extended family gets together for late evening mass. Then they gather for a whole night of celebration at one of their homes. There is a large full meal buffet, music and dancing. Someone plays the part of "Pére Noël" and everyone opens his gift. The children nap the afternoon before so they can stay up as late as they want and everyone sleeps most of Christmas Day.

– Patti Miller, St. Romuald, Québec

Enchiladas Navajo
(Mexican in origin but a favorite of Navajos)

Serves 10

Brown:
> ³/₄ lb. hamburger (or use chicken cooked and boned)
> 1 c. onion, chopped

Drain fat.
When onion is clear, add and simmer 15 minutes:
> 1 clove of garlic, minced or mashed
> 2 medium green chilies, skinned and chopped (may use canned)
> ³/₄ c. ripe olives, chopped
> 1 t. salt

Heat in 2 T. oil to soften (1 tortilla at a time):
> 10 corn tortillas, about 5-inch diameter

Drain quickly.
> 1 lb. jar picante sauce
> 8 oz. grated cheddar cheese

Put about ¹/₃ c. meat and sauce on tortilla. Sprinkle cheese on top. Heat at 350° about 10 minutes until the cheese melts.

Options:
Pour half the sauce in an ungreased baking dish. Place about ¹/₃ c. of meat mixture on each tortilla and roll to enclose filling. Place the flap side down in the sauce in the bottom of the dish. Pour the remaining sauce evenly over the tortillas. Cover with grated cheese. Bake uncovered at 350° until thoroughly heated.

Sauce option:
Cream of chicken or cream of mushroom soup may be added to the meat sauce along with chopped tomatoes, red peppers and vinegar.

– *Ernie Francisco, Bloomfield, NM*

Shrimp and Ground Pork Toast
Thailand

In a bowl mix:
>$^1/_2$ c. ground pork
>$^1/_2$ c. shrimp, shelled, cleaned and minced
>1 T. spring onion and coriander, finely chopped
>1 t. garlic salt
>$^1/_2$ t. pepper
>1 egg

Take 10 slices of old or stale bread. Cut in desired shapes (triangles or use cookie cutter). Spread the meat mixture over each piece of bread. Deep fry in 1 c. vegetable oil with meat mixture side down; turn over and continue cooking for 2 more minutes until brown. Drain on paper towel. Serve hot with 2 T. of hot sauce.

– Wannee Thompson, Manorom, Thailand

Sardine Bake
England

Serves 4

Arrange in a well-greased baking dish:
>1$^1/_2$ lb. sardines (bones and heads removed)

Sprinkle over sardines:
>salt and pepper to taste
>1 t. grated nutmeg

Cover with a layer of:
>3 tomatoes, skinned and sliced

Sprinkle over the above:
>1 onion, grated
>2 T. dry bread crumbs

Pour 2 oz. melted butter over the above. Preheat oven to 350°. Bake for 15 to 20 minutes or until the fish is cooked and flakes easily.

Serve with fresh bread.

– Judy Smith, London, England

In the Lamao Chapel it was common for people to carry their offering to the front to hand it to the pastor. One Sunday morning one of the older men, dressed in his appropriate G-string, got up slowly, and walked solemnly to the front, facing Pastor Sevilleja. He carefully reached within the folds of his loincloth, from which he pulled an egg, and gently placed it in the pastor's hands. That offering was about as memorable as the one Jesus watched at the gate of the temple in Jerusalem, when the poor widow put in her two mites.

*– J. Wilmer Heisey,
Mount Joy, PA
(MCC, Philippines)*

Broiled Trout
Cree

Serves 4-6

Fillet **1 trout, leaving skin intact.**
Place fillets skin side up in broiling pan.
Broil until skin is crusty and excess fat has dripped out.
Turn fillets flesh side up and **season with garlic salt and pepper to taste.**
Baste with **lemon juice and garnish with onion rings (optional).**
Brown and serve with **lemon wedges (optional) and tartar sauce (optional).**

Kami Ross's grandmother made many pairs of moccasins for staff at Timber Bay Children's Home.

– Kami Ross, Saskatchewan, Canada

Shrimp Curry
Thailand

On very low heat melt:
  1 T. butter
Stir in and cook until light brown:
  2 T. flour
Add and stir-fry on medium heat for 2 minutes:
  1 c. shrimp, shelled and cleaned
  1 T. onion, minced
Add and stir until thickened:
  1 T. curry powder
  salt to taste
  ¹/₂ c. milk
Add and cook for 3 minutes:
  2 small white onions, peeled
  2 potatoes, boiled and chopped
  1 carrot, boiled and cut into 1-inch
    segments
  2 chili peppers, cut into 1-inch segments
If you wish, add **2-3 drops yellow food coloring.**
Serve with **1 c. cooked rice.**

You may substitute chicken for shrimp and
coconut milk for milk. Add salt or sugar to taste.

– Wannee Thompson, Manorom, Thailand

Grilled Meat
Marinade
Honduras

Carne Asada
(CAR-nay Ah-SAH-dah)

Mix together:
  1 onion, diced
  ¹/₂ t. salt
  juice from 1 lemon
Place meat in this sauce and allow to marinate
for 2-3 hours. Grill over open flame, adding
sauce before turning.

– Yolanda Calderón de Herrera,
Tegucigalpa, Honduras

Shrimp Curry or Bengal Curry
India

Sauté **3 lb. medium shrimp, peeled and deveined, in 4 T. margarine or butter.** Sauté only a few at a time. Do not overcook. When they turn pink, set aside in a large bowl. Cut the following into bite size chunks and sauté about 10 minutes in shrimp pot, adding more butter as needed:

- ¹/₄ **c. celery**
- ¹/₄ **c. green pepper**
- ¹/₄ **c. onions**
- ¹/₄ **c. mushrooms**
- ¹/₄ **c. flaked coconut**

Set aside in same bowl with shrimp. In same pot, melt more butter then remove from heat. Add:

- **3-4 T. flour**
- **1 T. curry powder or to taste**
- **few drops Worcestershire sauce**
- **1 t. sugar**
- **1 t. vinegar**
- **salt and pepper to taste**

Return to low heat and stir in about 3 c. milk, a little at a time. Bring to boil over medium heat, stirring constantly. Add more milk if necessary to get the consistency you want. Add shrimp and vegetables and cook for a few minutes. Remove from heat and let shrimp curry rest. Before serving, add the following and heat thoroughly:

- **2 red apples, diced**
- ¹/₂ **c. raisins**

Serve over rice for evening meal. Add a side dish of chutney.

Curry powder is composed of cumin, turmeric, cardamom, coriander, mustard, saffron, and allspice. Chutney is to curry what barbecue sauce is to spareribs.

– Edna Kreider, Elizabethtown, PA (Bihar, India)

Sweet and Sour Fish
Thailand

Combine for marinade:
  2 T. sherry
  2 T. light soy sauce
  2 T. wheat flour
  2 T. corn flour
Pour marinade over:
  $1/2$ lb. fish, sliced into $1/2$-inch thick pieces
Heat 3 T. oil in deep pan.
Fry fish pieces until crisp and golden, then remove and drain.
In same oil fry for 1 minute:
  1 onion, sliced and separated into rings
  1 sweet pepper, sliced into $1/2$ x 2-inch strips
  1 carrot, cut into 2 x $1/2$ x $1/4$-inch pieces, and blanched in boiling water
Mix together for sauce:
  $1/3$ c. sugar
  $3/4$ c. tomato catsup
  $1/4$ c. vinegar
  4 T. sherry
Combine and stir into sauce:
  $1/2$ c. water
  $1^{1}/2$ T. corn flour
Pour sauce into frying pan and cook over low heat until thickened. Then add fish and vegetables, stirring together thoroughly. Spoon fish and sauce onto serving dish and surround with 2 pineapple rings, each cut into six pieces.

– Kathy Brubaker, Grantham, PA, (Bangkok, Thailand)

There's good fishing in troubled water.
– Spanish proverb

Sauce for Meats
Colombia

Adobo para Carnes
(a-DOH-boh pah-rah CAR-nays)

Chop all ingredients by hand or put all into the blender to combine:
- 1 large onion
- 1 stem leeks
- 1 medium carrot
- 1 bunch fresh thyme
- 1 stalk celery
- 1 bunch cilantro
- 1 bunch parsley
- 1 head of garlic
- $^1/_2$ T. cumin
- $^1/_2$ T. pepper
- 2 T. oil
- 2 t. salt

This is a seasoning for meat. It can be rubbed on meat before cooking or can be added to soups, meat or fish during cooking. This keeps well in a covered container in the refrigerator for several weeks.

– Elsa Cogua, Niza 9, Bogota, Colombia

Marinating Sauce
Japan

Combine in blender:
- 1$^1/_4$ c. soy sauce (Kikkoman)
- 3 T. mirin (sweetened rice wine)
- 2 cloves garlic
- 1 onion, cut in chunks
- 2 T. sesame seeds (optional)
- 2 t. fresh ginger, grated (optional)

Store in refrigerator.

This is a good sauce for any kind of meat, especially for mutton. Marinate for 30 minutes to remove that "muttony" taste.

– Kimiko Nishimura, Nagato, Japan

The jeep ride to Rajdhani, a distance of thirty miles, concluded with the usual bumps, dips and ruts of ox cart paths–our regular Sunday experience for worship visits in rural Bihar, India. But the welcome was warm from Puni's (pun-ee) mother. We knew her only as "Puni's Mother" for it was not uncommon for a parent to be known as somebody's father or mother among our Bihar Brethren in Christ. She first invited us to sit on the rope bed in the shade of her courtyard. Then, according to gracious Santal custom, she set a small brass pot of water in front of Harvey before extending her greeting. These missionaries, she knew, were younger than she, so she folded her hands together and drew them to her body in greeting. Harvey responded by bowing his head and extending his right hand, left hand placed on his right arm, but never touching her. Then it was my turn so I bowed before her, extending my hands almost to the ground. We were greeted properly and well! (Had we been older, she would have bowed to us. Between friends or guests of the same age, this greeting can bring forth laughter as guest and hostess try to force the other to bow.)

The local members had not yet arrived for worship in a neighbor's courtyard so we relaxed and chatted as we waited. Our hostess, a widow, was busy about something in her house–perhaps a cup of hot tea to revive us?

Time passed slowly as it always seemed to do on those Sunday mornings when we waited for folk to gather. Village life unfolded around us. Flies buzzed around our heads. Brain fever birds called for rain. Young herders set off for the day on the backs of the water buffalos. No one seemed in a hurry to gather, other than the missionaries!

Then our hostess sidled shyly from her kitchen, and we were invited into the enclosed porch of the Santal home and seated on a folded quilt on the floor. Shiny brass plates were placed in front of us. She took her big ladle and placed in the middle of the plate an abundant serving of rice (they would have been enormous had we not asked her to give us only small portions!). Soon she was back and this time with what appeared to be meat curry. She paused in her serving to ask the blessing. Appropriate comments were made as to how kind she was to think of preparing food for us, although we had an empty feeling in our hearts for we knew there would be less food for her family because we were fed so generously.

Thoughtfully left alone as we ate the extremely tasty meat curry, Harvey and I discussed what kind of meat it could possibly be. It wasn't fish, although the river was nearby. Certainly it wasn't goat meat for we ate that nearly every day and were well acquainted with the taste and texture. Finally, we settled on pork because we knew that many Santals keep a pig in their courtyard for trading or eating. Yet, it just didn't seem like pork either. Where could that lovely white meat with the one-half inch thick fat "on the side" have come from? Curiosity got the better of us so, telling the cook how good the food was and how much we were enjoying it, we asked just what kind of meat it was. Puni's mother was embarrassed immediately but after a few smiles and chuckles she told us that son Luke had been down at the river and, catching sight of an unsuspecting turtle, he brought it home for lunch!

For us, the memory of eating turtle meat served by that gracious Santal hostess has remained warm in our hearts. The spirit of hospitality in her heart overcame her timidity and embarrassment in serving the missionary something so humble as a lowly turtle. She gave what she had and we received it with joy, hospitality at its highest.

– Erma J. Sider,
Mechanicsburg, PA (Bihar, India)

On this mountain the L ORD Almighty will prepare a feast of rich food for all peoples, a banquet of aged wine – the best of meats and the finest of wines.

Isaiah 25:6

The theme of structural racism, and the church's response to it, is prominent today. Here in Cincinnati I am finding that one program really has potential for breaking down the walls between the races; develop relationships with people of other ethnic groups. Get to know others. These relationships should be based on genuine friendship and respect, not just on spiritual and social issues. Get to know others who are in a different economic position, whether more affluent or more needy than you. Forums for meeting others might include: developing a children's program that opens the doors to kids and their parents of other cultures; integrating different styles of music into a production; simply visiting your neighbors and inviting them to dinner in your home or in a restaurant; stopping to talk about significant things with the culturally different people that are already around you; eating in ethnic restaurants or learning to cook ethnic foods; joining in a service project or outreach opportunity with a culturally different church; taking a prayer walk through your community and greeting those you pass along the way (People like to talk. Start with small talk, then pass by there again later and reacquaint yourself, thus building a relationship.); attending culturally different events; teaming up with a Christian brother or sister of a different race to study the Bible together, one on one; moving into a neighborhood/community where cultural diversity exists.

– *Matthew Bye, Cincinnati, OH*

Serving rice – India

136

MAIN DISHES

"He offered her
some roasted
grain. She ate all
she wanted and
had some left
over."

—Ruth 2:14

Naomi took her daughter-in-law Ruth with her when she returned to Judah after the death of her husband. Arriving just as the barley harvest was beginning, Ruth went to the fields to try to glean grain left behind by the harvest workers. Boaz noticed her and extended his hospitality to her; not only did he offer her food and drink and allow her to glean in his fields, but he also promised her protection from workers who otherwise may have harmed her. His hospitality resulted in their marriage, and from their marriage came Obed who was the father of Jesse who was the father of David, and on down to Jesus Christ himself. Who knows what can happen when you offer grain to a stranger!

The situation of famine faced by Naomi and Ruth, precipitating their return to Judah, is one with which many people in various places in the world can identify at one time or another. Yet scientists tell us that "enough food is now produced worldwide to provide sufficient calories for all humans" (Microsoft Encarta Encyclopedia, 1996, Microsoft Corporation).

According to *U.S. News and World Report*, "the world's total grain harvest has risen steadily over the years" (Bob Holmes, "Feeding a World of 10 Billion," *USNWR*, February 8, 1993, p. 55). Improved seeds and fertilizers have increased corn and wheat production in Africa, while rice plants are being developed with less stems, more seeds and therefore greater yields. Barring insufficient rain, soil erosion and other environmental problems, political instability and/or lack of money, with hard work and scientific investment, the world's farmers can indeed produce enough food to feed everyone.

Main dishes without meat are often considered healthier. The traditional diets of Asia, for example, do not include much meat, and especially in rural areas where meat consumption is even lower, rates of such ailments as high cholestrol, heart disease, osteoporosis, cancer and diabetes are much lower than in countries where meat consumption is high. To get the benefits of an Asian diet, experts recommend "eating lots of grains, a good amount of fresh vegetables, legumes, soyfoods and fruit, and very little fat or animal-based foods, as people from India to Japan do" (Dana Jacobi, "The World's Healthiest Diet," Natural Health, January-February 1996, pp. 90ff.). When meat is used as part of a main dish, it is often used sparingly, like a garnish.

When you prepare your main dish from the recipes that follow, remember Boaz' gift of grain to Ruth and her mother-in-law, and remember the people all over the world for whom grains are the primary stuff of life.

Peanut Pie
Zimbabwe

Serves 8

Soak overnight:
   2 c. raw peanuts
In the morning, cook approximately 2 hours
until soft. Drain and chop coarsely. Set aside
until needed.
Combine in saucepan and cook until soft,
approximately 20-30 minutes:
   2 small onions, chopped
   2 medium tomatoes, chopped
   2 medium potatoes, diced
   1 t. salt
   2 c. water or enough to cover vegetables
Stir in chopped, cooked peanuts. Combine and
add to mixture:
   $^1/_2$ c. white corn meal
   $^1/_2$ c. cold water
Simmer 5 minutes. Pour mixture into 10–inch
deep pie pan. Sprinkle over the top:
   1 c. shredded cheese
Bake at 350° for 30 minutes until cheese is
melted and slightly browned.

This is a very satisfying vegetarian dish, full of
nutrients.

– Jester Mlilo, Bulawayo, Zimbabwe

I t takes courage to admit the insolubility of a problem and to strike out into the dark of contemplation, from which an eventual solution or an alternative situation may develop. It means to choose Mary, not Martha, when the kitchen is full of bubbling pots. But if we are busy fussing about the pots, we put in doubt the possibility of long-range solutions to the perpetual kitchen mess.

– Evelyn Mattern, "Some Thoughts on Mourning," Summer 1995 issue of Spiritual Life

Peanut Butter Gravy
Zimbabwe

Idobi
(Eh-DOH-bee)

Serves 6

Saute in ¹/₄ c. margerine:
  ¹/₄ c. onions, chopped
Add and stir to make smooth paste:
  ¹/₄ c. flour
  ¹/₂ t. salt
Mix together, and add to above:
  1 c. peanut butter
  1 c. warm water
Add and heat to boiling:
  3 c. milk
  10 oz. frozen spinach, thawed and drained
Continue stirring to keep gravy smooth. Serve with thick corn meal porridge.

– Erma Hoover, Mechanicsburg, PA

Weddings

When we lived at Macha, I became somewhat famous for making long white wedding dresses for many of our Christian brides. The catch about this was — I was hardly ever able to fit them on the bride. In Zambian culture, the bridegroom plans and pays for all the wedding expenses, including the bride's and bridesmaids' attire. Often the material and the pattern would be brought to me but since it was taboo for the engaged couple to talk or be together until after marriage, I had to guess about the fit. Most people in the villages in those days didn't have tape measures, let alone rulers or yardsticks, so the groom would tell me what the bride looked like. Sometimes a relative or friend of the bride of a similar size would be sent for me to fit the wedding dress. It was amazing how everything fit on the wedding day!

– Ardys Thuma, Bradford, OH (Macha, Zambia)

Chili Beans
Navajo
(Mexican not
Navajo in origin
but a favorite)

Soak overnight and cook until tender:
   3 c. dry pinto beans
In another pan brown:
   1 lb. hamburger
Then add and cook until golden:
   $^1/_2$ c. onions, chopped
Add:
   2 c. whole tomatoes
   1 or 2 T. red chili peppers
   2 t. salt
Simmer for 15 minutes and add:
   2 medium size green chilies (broil or roast,
skin, seed, and chop)
Drain the beans, reserving the liquid, then add
them to the tomato mixture along with 2 c. of the
reserved liquid. Cover and simmer for an hour.

–Faye Francisco, Bloomfield, NM

Breakfast Grace
Be present at our table, Lord,
Be here and everywhere adored;
These mercies bless, and grant that we
May live and work today with Thee.
We thank Thee, Lord, for this our food,
For life, and health, and every good.
Let manna to our souls be given
The Bread of Life sent down from heaven. Amen.

Black Beans
Venezuela

Frijoles Negros
(Free-HO-lays
NAY-gross)

Rinse and cook in 2 quarts water for 2 minutes:

2 c. (1 lb.) black beans

Cover kettle, remove from heat and let sit for 1 hour. Drain. Add 1¹/₂ quarts water to the beans and cook without salt until tender, approximately 2 hours. Do not drain after cooking.
Season with:

1 onion, chopped
1 small red or green sweet pepper, chopped
1 clove garlic, minced,
     or garlic powder to taste
cumin to taste (optional)
salt
several sprigs fresh cilantro (optional)

Continue cooking until flavor has penetrated beans, approximately ¹/₂ hour. Beans should be very soft and the juice thick.

Serve with rice.

This can be prepared a couple of days in advance and reheated.
Red beans may be used instead of black beans.
May use canned beans.
Cumin and cilantro are not essential but are used frequently in Latin American cooking and add a good flavor. Cumin is found in the spice section. Cilantro is found in some supermarkets or small groceries where Spanish-speaking people shop. It looks like flat–leaf parsley and is found in the fresh vegetable area.

– Thata Book, Manheim, PA (Cagua, Venezuela)

Offer hospitality to one another without grumbling. Each one should use whatever gift he has received to serve others, faithfully administering God's grace in its various forms.

– 1 Peter 4:9,10

Refried Beans
Navajo

Soak overnight:
  1 lb. pinto beans,
Drain beans. Add:
  6 c. water
  2 onions, chopped
  Salt to taste
Cook until tender. Mash with potato masher. Hot sauce, chili powder, tomato sauce, and bacon can be added. Cook in heavy skillet until beans are thickened and juices are absorbed.

– Karen Redfearn, New Mexico

Refried Beans
Nicaragua

Frijoles Licuados
(Free-HO-lays Lee-KWAH-dohs)

Serves about 5

Liquefy in blender:
  2 c. cooked pinto beans
  ¹/₄ c. chopped onion
  ¹/₄ c. chopped green pepper
Heat small amount oil in frying pan. Add bean mixture and cook over low heat, stirring constantly for about 5 minutes. Add any desired seasonings, such as hot sauce, salt, and chili powder.

Serving suggestions: with rice as part of a meal, as dip on tortilla chips, on crackers with a little sour cream, or on crackers with an olive slice.

Option: Use canned red or black beans.

– Perla Estrada, Managua, Nicaragua

Come, all you who are thirsty, come to the waters; and you who have no money, come, buy and eat! Come, buy wine and milk without money and without cost.

– Isaiah 55:1

M enu for Day One: Rice and curry for lunch. Rice and curry for dinner. Menu for Day Two: Rice and curry for lunch. Rice and curry for dinner. And so it went for most of the 25 days of our visit to India. And we loved it!

We were the guests of our Indian brothers and sisters, first at the Mennonite World Conference (MWC) in Calcutta, and then at the International Brethren in Christ Fellowship (IBICF) in Purnea, Bihar. Our hosts at MWC treated their 4,000 plus guests royally. Food was abundant and delicious, especially for those of us who during ministry in India had grown to enjoy the fragrant Basmati rice and mouth tingling curries. Young volunteers from churches throughout the country served the long lines of foreigners and Indians joyfully and efficiently.

At IBICF the hospitality, while on a smaller scale, was just as bountiful. We were given the best of everything: the best of food with meat curry once a day; the best hotel for sleeping with warm water delivered to our door twice a day; the best bus in Bihar for transportation. Comparatively speaking, we 41 visitors from overseas lived like kings and queens.

– Erma J. Sider, Mechanicsburg, PA (Bihar, India)

Yorkshire Pudding *England*

Serves 4

Sift into a bowl:
   ¹/₂ c. flour
Make a well in the center and add:
   2 eggs
   ¹/₂ t. salt
   ¹/₄ c. of milk.
Beat gradually to a smooth batter, adding **³/₄ c. milk** as the mixture blends together. (Alternately, put everything into a blender and blend at top speed until smooth.) Chill for one hour. Put an 8-inch x 8-inch pan into a hot oven (400° - 450°) with **¹/₄ c. shortening.** When very hot, add batter after stirring it several times. Although this may require baking for 30-40 minutes, check after 20 minutes. They are best crisp and brown.

Serve with roast beef or mutton.

– Judy Smith, London, England

Pinto Beans
Navajo

Serves 6

Clean and wash beans; cover with water. Either let beans soak overnight or bring to a boil for 2 minutes, cover kettle, remove from heat and let cool 1 hour:

1 lb. dry pinto beans
6 c. water

Add the following ingredients to the beans, cover, and cook slowly for $1^1/2$ - 2 hours until tender:

salt pork, bacon, or pork butt
1 bell pepper
1 whole onion
1 hot pepper (jalapeño - seeded and finely chopped)
$^1/_4$ t. black pepper

Add to the above ingredients and cook over low fire in open pot until juice is thick, stirring occasionally:

1 t. salt
2 T. sugar, molasses, or honey

Pinto beans are favorites always to be found at a pot luck but it can be served anywhere.

– Lydia Adcock, New Mexico

A water pot that is half-full is full of noisy splashes but of little value.

– Indian proverb

One Pot Meal
Nepal

Pani Roti
(PAH-nee ROH-tee)

Clean and soak overnight:
  2 c. dried peas
  2 c. mung peas (green gram)
  2 c. navy beans
  2 c. chick peas
In a heavy saucepan heat:
  1 T. oil
  1 t. ground cumin
  1 t. ground coriander
  $1/4$ t. black pepper.
Add and sauté lightly:
  prepared lentils (peas, etc.)
  4 large potatoes, sliced
Add:
  3 c. water
  1 t. salt
Cover and simmer gently for about 15 minutes.
Add and simmer gently 2-3 minutes:
  1 package spinach, chopped
  $1/2$ t. turmeric

While above is cooking, prepare pastry:
Knead:
  1 c. whole wheat flour
  2-3 T. water or enough to dampen and form
  in a ball
Knead for two or three minutes and roll out thin
(like potpie). Cut in small squares. Make sure
there is enough water in the stew and drop in the
squares separately. Boil for another 15 minutes or
so, until the dough is cooked.

– Esther Lenhert, Kathmandu, Nepal

Belly full, heart happy.

– Spanish proverb

Hummus
Jordan

Mash:
    15¹/₂-oz. can chick peas, drained
Add slowly to above:
    1 c. tahini
    1 c. lemon juice
Mix well.

Options:
I have sometimes substituted peanut butter for tahini as it gives a little different flavor.
Use baking soda if cooking dried peas.
Salt may be added as desired.

In the Mideast, hummus is served in a bowl or plate and drizzled with olive oil and a few whole chick peas for garnish. Each person tears off a bite-size piece of pita bread from the whole round piece, scoops up some hummus with the bread and—enjoys!

Tahini is available in Middle Eastern stores.

– Ethel Kreider, Lancaster, PA (Jordan)

Hominy and Chick Peas
Zimbabwe

Isimoni
(Eh-sih-MOH-nee)

Serves 4

Combine in saucepan and bring to a boil:
    1 c. hominy (grits)
    2 c. canned chick peas, drained
Stir in and simmer 3-5 minutes:
    ¹/₄ c. peanut butter
    ¹/₄ t. salt
Serve as a meat substitute.

– Martha Mpofu, Dekezi, Zimbabwe

Garbanzo Stew
Spain

Serves 6-8

Soak 1 lb. garbanzo beans (chick peas) overnight. Discard soaking water. In a large soup pot, crock pot, or pressure cooker combine:

soaked beans
ham bone or hock
1 lb. Spanish sausage (chorizo)
1-2 slices bacon, chopped
1 onion, chopped
2 carrots, cut in chunks
1 red sweet pepper, chopped
4 cloves of garlic, peeled
$^1/_2$ t. paprika
1 t. salt
$^1/_4$ t. pepper
water to cover

Cook until tender. Remove fat and cut meat into small pieces. Serve with fresh, hot bread.

– A.J. Mann, Elizabethtown, PA

Groundnuts in the Tonga Culture

Groundnuts are a very important part of the Tonga diet. Many people complain that they "have not really eaten" unless groundnuts (usually pounded) have been added to the relish (i.e. cooked vegetable) which they eat with insima (cooked cornmeal). The presence of groundnuts is a source of pride, especially to the Tonga grandmother.

The older women encourage the younger women to plant their own fields of groundnuts so that they may provide well for their families. Groundnuts provide the protein which may be lacking if there is financial stress and meat is unaffordable.

– Cindy Chisolm, Cumberland, MD (Macha, Zambia)

Potato Spanish Omelet
Spain

Tortilla Española

Serves 8

Thinly slice **4-5 medium potatoes.**
Heat 2 T. of olive oil in skillet to very hot. Add potatoes and cover. Check every couple of minutes to ensure they don't stick together and burn on edges.
    Beat 6 eggs in separate bowl.
    Add salt and pepper to taste.
As potatoes soften add:
    2 T. onions, chopped
Cook for 2-3 minutes more. Strain potatoes and add to eggs. Let sit for 15-20 minutes. Mash potatoes into egg mixture. Prepare another medium-size skillet making it very hot. Add egg and potato mixture to skillet. Turn heat down right away. When it begins to thicken, flip it using a large plate. Slide it back into the skillet. Flip 2 or 3 more times until it's firm.

May serve as an appetizer by cutting it into squares and picking it up with toothpicks or as a light supper cut in wedges and served with a salad.

– Merly Bundy, Madrid, Spain

Grilled Cheese and Tomatoes
Malawi

Serves 4-6

4 ripe tomatoes, sliced
1 c. grated cheese
salt and pepper
Arrange sliced tomatoes on a wire rack.
Add 1 T. cheese on top of each tomato slice.
Sprinkle with salt and pepper.
Bake for 10 minutes at 400° or until cheese melts.
Note: put cookie sheet under to catch drippings from tomatoes.
Garnish with parsley.
Serve immediately.

– Mel Andricks, Blantyre, Malawi

Egg Curry
India

(AHN-dah KAH-ree)

Serves 4-6

Hard boil and cut in half lengthwise:
  8 eggs
Sauté in **¼ c. vegetable oil** until onions are golden:
  2 medium onions, minced
  1 t. marjoram
  1 t. thyme
Add and cook, stirring constantly, for 3 to 4 minutes:
  1 t. turmeric
  1½ t. salt
  2 t. dried, unsweetened coconut
  1 T. curry powder
  1 T. parsley flakes
Next add:
  4 large tomatoes, sliced
  1 c. yogurt
Stir well, then add eggs being careful not to break them. Cover, lower heat and allow to simmer for 10 minutes.

Serve as a main dish with rice.

– Ken Hoke, Carlisle, PA

"Lord, when did we see you hungry and feed you, or thirsty and give you something to drink? When did we see you a stranger and invite you in, or needing clothes and clothe you? When did we see you sick or in prison and go to visit you?"

The king will reply, "I tell you the truth, whatever you did for one of the least of these brothers of mine, you did for me."

– Matthew 25:37

Fried Noodles
Thai Style
Thailand

Heat 3 T. oil in a frying pan and sauté:
   1 T. garlic, chopped
   1 T. shallots, chopped
When yellow, add:
   12 oz. narrow rice noodles
Fry, turning constantly with spatula to prevent sticking. Then move noodles to side or remove from pan.
Heat 2–3 T. oil in pan and add:
   $1/2$ c. pork, cut into small slivers
   $1/2$ c. pickled white radish, chopped
   1 cake soybean curd, cut into small slivers
   1 t. dried chilies, ground
Return the noodles to the pan, mix thoroughly, and move to side or remove.
Heat 2 T. oil in the pan.
Break into pan and scramble with spatula, spreading in a thin layer:
   3 eggs
When set, return the noodles and mix together with the following sauce:
   4 T. sugar
   3 T. fish sauce
   4 T. tamarind juice or vinegar
Add:
   1 pack bean sprouts
   $1/2$ c. Chinese leek leaves
Turn to mix together.
Spoon onto plates and sprinkle with:
   $1/2$ c. roasted peanuts, ground

– Kathy Brubaker, Bangkok, Thailand

German Hot Potato Salad
Pennsylvania/ German

Warmer Kartoffelsalat
(VEHR-mer ker-JOFF-el sah-laht)

Serves 10-12

This is delicious served any time of year. When our family/children return home for a visit and discover potato salad is on the menu, their expressed hope is that it will be Warmer Kartoffelsalat.

Boil, peel and slice thinly ($1/8$-inch - $1/4$-inch):
  12 medium potatoes in jackets
In skillet fry until crisp:
  12 slices of bacon
Remove bacon and drain on paper towel.
Crumble and set aside.
Save drippings in a one-cup measure.
Sauté until golden brown:
  2-3 medium onions, diced
  1 t. bacon drippings
Remove onions, add to potatoes with:
  1 c. celery, thinly sliced
  parsley, snipped
To bacon drippings add enough salad oil to make 1/2 cup. Pour into skillet.
Add:
  1 c. sugar
  5 T. flour
  2-3 t. salt
  $1/2$ t. ground black pepper
  1 t. celery seed
Stir until smooth. Continue cooking for 3 minutes.
Pour dressing over potato mixture.
Add crumbled bacon. Mix thoroughly and carefully.
Keep warm until ready to serve or serve at room temperature.
Garnish with thinly sliced hard-boiled egg and sweet green pepper rings.

– Faithe Hoffman, Palmyra, PA

Ye be as full of good manners as an egg of oatmeal.

– English proverb

Crumbs
Colombia

Serves 4-6

Soak 4-6 **tortillas in 1-2 c. of milk** (or just enough to soak tortillas well) for at least 30 minutes or until they fall apart easily. With your hands, divide these into small pieces and continue to soak in the milk.

In a skillet, fry in small amount of oil:

1 onion, finely chopped
3 tomatoes, finely chopped

Cook until most of the liquid of the tomatoes is gone.

Beat **4-6 eggs** and mix with tortilla/milk mixture. Add this mixture to skillet and cook. Add salt to taste.

Options: Other types of breads can be used in place of tortillas.

Garlic powder and hot sauce are optional.

A practical guide is to use 1 tortilla and 1 egg per person. Can vary from 4-6 without changing onion or tomato.

This is a common breakfast for some regions of Colombia. Good for a lunch or evening meal with tossed salad and fruit.

– *Tatiana Mallarino Giraldo, Niza 9, Vila Nova,*
Bogota, Colombia

W hen a woman has a baby, the other women from her village and nearby villages help with providing food for the family. They come bringing mealie rice, relish and usually green vegetables. Some of this food is cooked and some uncooked. The reason for this is that the woman is supposed to rest and not do her cooking and other household duties for about three weeks after delivery.

–Ann Marie Parry,
Danville, PA
(Choma, Zambia)

153

Cornmeal Porridge
Zambia

Insima
(En-SHEE-mah)

Serves 4-6

5 c. water
1¹/₂ - 2 c. white cornmeal
Bring 4 c. water to a boil in large heavy saucepan. Slowly add to the boiling water 1 c. cornmeal that has been mixed with 1 c. water. As you add the cornmeal mixture, stir vigorously with a wooden spoon to keep from getting lumps. Slowly add another ¹/₂ - 1 c. cornmeal to mixture on the stove, again stirring vigorously and continuously with wooden spoon. When cornmeal mixture seems very thick, it is time to stop adding more cornmeal. Cover and simmer ¹/₂ - ³/₄ hour, stirring occasionally and vigorously with wooden spoon. It is ready to eat when it no longer tastes like raw cornmeal.

Options:
Zambians do not put salt in their insima, because they heavily salt the chicken or other relish eaten with it. However, since I usually add just normal amounts to the chicken or other relish, I add 1 t. salt to the boiling water in the beginning.

This should serve 4-6 Americans; double it for 8-12 people. If you have any left over, flatten into loaf pan. Make fried mush (Pennsylvania Dutch style) for breakfast or lunch.

This is a staple food of most Zambians and is very good with Tonga Chicken.

– Ardys E. Thuma, Bradford, OH
(Hamaseele, Choma, Zambia)

He [God] defends the cause of the fatherless and the widow, and loves the alien, giving him food and clothing.

– Deuteronomy 10:18

Cornmeal Porridge
Zimbabwe

Sadza (SUH-dzah)
or
Isitshwala
(Eh-seh-CHWAH-lah)

Serves 4

Boil in saucepan:
  3 c. water
Combine:
  1 c. white cornmeal
  1 c. cold water
Stir mixture into boiling water. Stir constantly until porridge boils and thickens. Cover, lower heat, and cook for 5 - 10 minutes.
Add gradually while stirring:
  $1/2$ c. dry cornmeal
Stir porridge constantly to keep it smooth. Cover and simmer for an additional 5-10 minutes. Serve with Zimbabwean Stew, Peanut Butter Gravy, Cabbage with Peanut Butter or any similiar recipe.

This is the staple dish served in Zimbabwe, and may be served twice a day.

– Boitatelo Mguni, Zimbabwe,
Fadzai Moyo, London, U.K.

Mixed Grain Dish
Zimbabwe

Soak overnight:
  1 c. raw peanuts
Drain water, add fresh water to cover peanuts, cook for about 2 hours.
To cooked peanuts, add:
  2 c. hominy
  1 c. kidney beans, canned
  1 c. chick peas, canned
  $1/2$ t. salt
Simmer gently for 15 - 20 minutes. Serve as main course of the meal.

Serve with vegetable or salad for a complete meal. It is very ideal for developing countries where meat may be difficult to get.

– Beatrice Ncube, Dekezi, Zimbabwe

Spanish Paella
Spain

Heat $^1/_2$ c. olive oil in heavy pan and sauté until brown then set aside:

2-3 lb. chicken pieces, cut in small pieces

Then in the same pan sauté, stirring frequently:

6 large shrimp, shelled and deveined

Remove from pan and reserve.

Steam in a little water until they open, then drain, reserving juices:

12 mussels in shells, scrubbed

12 small clams in shells, scrubbed

In remaining oil sauté:

1 large onion, chopped

1 clove garlic, minced

Add **2 c. rice** and cook, lightly stirring until grains are coated with oil. Put rice in a shallow 12-14–inch paella pan. As evenly as possible arrange shrimp, chicken, 1 **tomato** peeled and chopped, 1 10 oz. package of **frozen peas** over the rice. Measure clam and mussel broth and add enough water to make $4^1/_2$ c. Add 5 c. chicken broth. Bring to a boil.

Stir in:

2 t. salt to taste

$^1/_2$ **t. ground saffron**

Heat the paella pan and pour the hot broth over the rice. Cook over moderately high heat for 10 minutes. Reduce heat to medium and cook 15 minutes longer, until rice is tender and liquid is absorbed. Arrange clams and mussels, still in shells, on top.

Option: Parsley and lemon juice add flavor and zest.

– Merly Bundy, Madrid, Spain

Rice Quiche
Japan

Serves 4

Fry and then set aside:
>   **2 slices bacon, chopped**
Fry together in bacon fat and **1-2 t. butter:**
>   **1 onion, minced**
>   **1 clove garlic, minced**
>   **1 red pepper, chopped**
>   **1 green pepper, chopped**
Mix and place in buttered baking dish:
>   **2 c. cooked rice**
>   **1 c. raw squash, cubed**
>   **fried bacon**
>   **1 T. parsley, minced**
>   **³/₄ t. salt**
>   **dash pepper/dash nutmeg (optional)**
Beat together and pour over rice mixture:
>   **4 eggs**
>   **1 c. evaporated milk**
>   Top with **¹/₄ c. grated cheese.**
Bake at 350° for about 40 minutes or until set.

– Mariko Kogoma, Tokyo, Japan

Rice
England

Serves 12

Measure **3 c. long grain** rice into large saucepan, wash with cold water and drain. (Do not wash enriched or converted rice.)
Add:
>   **6 c. boiling water**
>   **1 t. salt**
Cover and boil on medium heat for 20 minutes.

Serve with stew or curry for lunch or the evening meal.

Option: To **3 c. rice** in saucepan add **5¹/₂ c. cold water**. Bring to a rapid boil. Turn heat to very low. Cover and cook until rice is dry, 30-40 minutes. Leave lid on for 10 more minutes. Stir with fork to fluff. For curries, basmati rice is preferred.

– Fadzai Moyo, London, U.K.

Rice Balls and Soy Bean Pods with Fish
Japan

A. **Rice balls**: 2 c. cooked rice (not instant). To make rice balls: wet hands and sprinkle generously with salt. Take a large spoonful of cooked rice and press firmly into a ball so it holds together in your hands. May sprinkle the rice balls with sesame seeds, or wrap ball in a square of sea weed.

B. **Bean pods**: wash and boil in heavily salted water 15-20 minutes.

To eat the beans squeeze the beans out of the pod right into your mouth. You end up with a big pile of pods on the plate, but what a treat!

C. **Fish**: bake or fry several pieces for each person.

Edible soy beans are still a favorite of our now grown children, and our mouths still water for those beans. Occasionally we've found seeds, and grown our own in our Pennsylvania garden. Our children's favorite picnic lunch in Japan was a huge pan of cooked (edible) soy beans (in the pod), rice balls and just-caught and fried-on-the-spot fish. When we were in the mountains on vacation we would go to a fish farm, catch our fish and have it cleaned and fried right there. A large pan of cooked soy beans and/or container of rice balls would complete our meal.

– Mary Willms, Camp Hill, PA (Hagi, Japan)

The jailer brought them [Paul and Silas] into his house and set a meal before them; he was filled with joy because he had come to believe in God–he and his whole family.

–Acts 16:34

Spanish Rice Pie
Spain

Serves 6-8

Cook **2 packages of frozen spinach** for 5 minutes and squeeze dry.
Fry in 5 T. oil:
   1 clove garlic, minced
   1 medium onion, chopped
   ¹/₂ t. salt
   dash of pepper
Mix and beat lightly:
   4 eggs
   5 T. grated Italian cheese
   ¹/₄ c. milk
   2¹/₂ T. grated Mozzarella cheese
Add all other ingredients and mix well:
   1 c. cooked rice
   Pinch crushed red pepper
Fill a greased 10-inch pie pan and bake at 375°
for ¹/₂ hour until lightly brown. Bake 10 minutes
more after sprinkling 2¹/₂ T. of grated Mozzarella
on top.

– A. J. Mann, Elizabethtown, PA

Spanish Rice
Navajo

Serves 4

Brown and drain:
   1 lb. ground beef
Chop and brown:
   1 medium onion
   ¹/₂ green bell pepper
Add:
   1 c. rice
   1 c. tomatoes
   2 t. salt
   1 t. chili powder
   2 c. water
Cover tightly, lower heat and cook slowly for 30
minutes or until the rice is cooked.

A favorite that can be eaten anywhere.

– John Jarred, Dzith na o Dilthe Le, NM

Lentils, Macaroni and Rice
Egypt

Kusheri
(Kush-r-EE)

Cook separately, adding salt to taste
- 1 c. rice
- 1 c. macaroni
- 1 c. lentils

In 2 t. oil sauté and set aside for garnish:
- **1 large onion, chopped**

Tomato Sauce:

In 2 T. hot oil sauté and set aside:
- **1 large onion, chopped**
- **2-3 cloves garlic, minced**

Add and simmer 5-10 minutes:
- **3 tomatoes, chopped**
- **¹/₂ t. salt**
- **1 c. water**
- **black pepper to taste, or hot red pepper**

Remove from heat and add **1 T. vinegar**

Serve in individual bowls starting with rice, then macaroni, then lentils. Cover with tomato sauce and top with sprinkling of fried onions.

This is a favorite vegetarian dish served in many restaurants or roadside stands.

– Brian and Marcelle Zook, Egypt

E ach year after the harvest, the Brethren in Christ churches in Zambia designate one or two Sundays for a harvest offering. The congregation is encouraged to contribute a tenth of their harvest for the work of the church and as a thank offering to God for the blessings He has bestowed on them.

– Ann Marie Parry,
Danville, PA
(Choma, Zambia)

Rice and Lentils
Nepal

Khichidi
(KICH-ree)

Into **5 c. boiling water** add:
¹/₂ c. black gram lentils
After it reaches boiling point again, add:
¹/₄ t. tumeric
¹/₄ t. asafoetida
Cover and simmer until the lentils are soft (may add more water if too thick).
Add:
1 c. rice and simmer until the rice is cooked.
Add:
1 t. oil
¹/₂ t. ginger
1 t. salt
Serve hot for a nourishing but light meal.

– Esther Lenhert , Kathmandu, Nepal

Spinach and Rice Pondo
Zaire

Serves 6

Cook together in saucepan:
2 packages of frozen spinach, chopped
or the equivalent of fresh spinach, chopped
1 medium onion, chopped
Drain excess liquid.
Add and stir over low heat until blended:
¹/₂ c. smooth peanut butter
2 t. hot pepper sauce - or more to taste
dash of salt

Serve as a main dish over 4-6 c. hot, cooked rice.

Variations: add cooked corn or any cooked meat, chopped.

This is one of the staple dishes of northern Zaire which Zairians enjoy spicy hot. I like to serve it as a vegetarian meal.

– Lucille Charlton, Vancouver, BC (Zaire)

Rice with Red Pork
Thailand

Marinate ¹/₂ lb. pork tenderloin in this sauce for several hours:

> 6 oz. can tomato paste
> 1¹/₂ c. water
> ¹/₄ c. soy sauce
> 2 T. sugar

Bake, covered, until tender. May baste and broil at end to lightly brown outside.

Slice ¹/₄ inch thick.

Arrange pork and cucumbers attractively on plates of rice. Thicken pan juices with flour mixed with water and pour over meat and 3-4 cucumbers (sliced ¹/₄-inch thick).

Garnish with fresh coriander leaves (cilantro).

Optional sauce:

> 2 T. sugar
> 2 T. vinegar
> 2 T. soy sauce

Mix together and add chilies sliced into thin rings.

– Kathy Brubaker, Grantham, PA
(Bangkok, Thailand)

Fried Rice Central Java, Indonesia

Nasi goreng
(NAH-see goh-reng)

Serves 6

Javanese people serve this for breakfast usually at room temperature, but I like to serve it piping hot. It is great with shrimp-flavored chips and available at international food stores.
I serve this dish most often for a quick dinner/supper. This is a great dish for using leftover rice since the key to successful fried rice is starting with cold rice. It's so energy and time efficient and provides a creative way of disguising leftover vegetables that collect in the refrigerator. We love it.

Measure into rice cooker or pan:
  2 c. rice
  3³/₄ - 4 c. cold water
Cook rice in cooker following directions or bring rice and water to boil in pan. Stir to loosen rice from bottom. When mixture boils, lower heat to warm. Cover. Do not peek for 20 minutes. Turn off heat, remove lid, cool, preferably for a number of hours. Rice must be cold.
Prepare the following ingredients for stir fry:
  1 large onion, chopped
  3 cloves garlic, sliced
  1 c. steamed broccoli or left-over green
    vegetables (i.e. peas, celery)
  2-3 T. cooking oil
  1 deboned chicken breast, julienned
  2 t. cumin
  soy sauce
Pour oil into wok. Add chicken with a few slices garlic. Stir fry until no pink remains. Sprinkle 1 t. cumin over mixture. Remove chicken.
Add and stir fry the onion, remaining garlic, 1 more t. cumin, a shake of soy sauce.
Gradually add rice (fluff with fork first to separate grains), stirring constantly. Return chicken strips to wok. Add green vegetables, soy sauce to taste. Stir fry until heated through and serve piping hot.

Suggested optional garnishes:
  2 shallots, sliced and fried
  ¹/₂ - 1 t. red hot pepper paste, stirring into
    fried rice at end
  1 egg sheet
Prepare egg sheet as follows: Beat egg and pour into wok, tipping wok to make thin sheet as it fries in a bit of oil. Lift with spatula, roll up, slice ¹/₄" wide.

– Shirlee Kohler Yoder, Harrisonburg, VA
(Central Java, Indonesia)

Mashed Potatoes
Egypt

Boil, peel and mash:
  6 potatoes
Add and mix thoroughly:
  1 c. milk
  pinch of salt and pepper
  2 eggs
In a skillet fry:
  1 large onion, diced.
Add and cook until brown:
  2 lb. ground beef
  pinch of salt and pepper
Beat and set aside:
  1 egg
Put half of potato mixture in baking pan. Cover with a layer of meat mixture. Then add the other half of the potato mixture and top with the beaten egg. Bake at 350° for 45 minutes or until brown.

– Brian and Marcelle Zook, Egypt

We visited our son Brian Zook for two weeks while he was serving with MCC in Egypt. We were invited into the home of Mr. and Mrs. Tawfik where we were treated to a special meal of stuffed pigeon, mashed potatoes with beef and bishemal.

– Ruth Zook,
Mechanicsburg, PA

Baked Stuffed Zucchini
Egypt

Macaroni Cosa Bishemal
(MAK-a-ROW-nah coh-SAH bell-bish-eh-MALL)

Serves 8

Make a white sauce using:
> ¹/₄ c. oil or butter
> 3 T. flour
> salt and pepper to taste
> 2 c. milk

Cook gently until thick. Cool.
Cook in boiling water until soft on the inside, but not well done:
> 8 medium to large zucchini

Slice zucchini lengthwise and remove middle.
Brush 9x13-inch pan with oil and put 8 halves in the pan.
Fill each half with the following meat mixture cooked well:
> 1 med. onion, chopped and fried in 1-2 T. oil
> 1 lb. beef, minced
> salt and pepper to taste (optional: hot pepper, cumin, parsley, paprika)

When stuffed, cover each zucchini with the other half.
Add to sauce and mix well:
> 2 eggs

Cover the zucchini with white sauce.
Bake at 350° until brown.

Usually eaten as a main meal with salad as a side dish.

Options: Cooked macaroni can be substituted for the zucchini. Add tin of crushed tomatoes to minced beef and cook until tomatoes are thick and dark. Layer macaroni, and meat/tomato mixture. Top with white sauce and bake until brown.

– Amal, Egypt

Tofu Patties
Japan

In a cheesecloth bag, squeeze water from:
>   2 squares tofu

Mash together in bowl with tofu:
> $^1/_2$ c. carrot, minced
> $^1/_2$ c. mushrooms, chopped
>   1 t. salt
>   1 T. sugar
>   dash of Accent

Add and mix well:
>   1 beaten egg

Shape into patties and fry in enough oil to cover patties.

Serve with mustard and soy sauce.

– Lucille Graybill, Osaka, Japan

Tofu Sauce for Vegetables
Japan

On a cloth-covered cutting board, drain for $^1/_2$ hour:
>   1 square tofu

Place in blender with tofu:
>   3 T. sesame seeds

Blend; add the following and blend thoroughly:
>   1 T. sugar
>   1 t. Accent
>   1 t. soy sauce

Pour over cooked vegetables.

– Lucille Graybill, Osaka, Japan

Eating is the pillar of the stomach.

– Tonga proverb

Scrambled Tofu on Rice
Japan

Place in cheese cloth bag and drain:
   1 square tofu
Brown in 1 T. oil:
   ¹/₂ lb. ground beef
   ¹/₂ c. carrots, slivered
   2 scallions, chopped
   4-5 sprigs parsley, minced
Scramble tofu as you add to meat and vegetables.
Stir in:
   3 T. soy sauce
   ¹/₂ t. salt
   1 T. sugar
   dash of Accent
Add and cook until eggs are set:
   2 slightly beaten eggs
Serve over rice in bowls

– Lucille Graybill, Lusaka, Japan

Dipping Sauce for Tofu
Japan

Soy sauce
dash of Accent
Fresh ginger, grated or white radish, grated

Tofu, prepared from soy beans, is an excellent source of protein. One-quarter pound is equivalent to a glass of milk or a very large egg. Tofu can be prepared in many ways: boiled, fried, stewed, or as a sauce and can be combined with vegetables, meats, and fish. It is very bland so it is necessary to use seasonings.

– Lucille Graybill, Osaka, Japan

Pepian
California
Spanish

Fry together:
  1 lb. tomatoes, chopped
  1 chili pepper, sliced
  1 medium onion, chopped
  2 cloves garlic, minced
Toast together:
  $^1/_2$ oz. sesame seed
  $^1/_2$ oz. rice
  3 whole cloves or $^1/_4$ t. ground cloves
  5 pepper corns
  1 stick cinnamon or 1 t. ground cinnamon
  3 slices of bread toasted until they are a
little burned in order to give a darker color.
Mix all the above in a blender, and heat gently in
1 t. oil.
Add:
  1 lb. of cooked beef, pork or chicken.
Season with salt to taste. Add a bundle of cilantro
and cook gently for a few minutes.

A good stew to serve with rice.

– Maria Arias, Cristo La Roca Church, Ontario, CA

Jesus said to them, "I tell you the truth; it is my Father who
gives you the true bread from heaven."

– John 6:32

Desserts

DESSERTS

"practice
hospitality"

—Romans 12

Typically, desserts eaten at the end of a meal leave a sweet taste in one's mouth and the memory of good food and good company. One of the lingering sweet tastes, metaphorically speaking, from a trip to Bolivia a number of years ago is of a visit with a group of Indian women deep in the heartland. Six out of nine people on a Mennonite Central Committee study tour traveled from Santa Cruz with our host and guide by Jeep over rough terrain and roads made almost impassable by recent heavy rains. About ten kilometers from El Carmen, our destination for the day, we were unable to go any further and had to get out and walk the rest of the way in intense afternoon heat and humidity. I was fortunate to be offered a ride on a motorcycle for the last few kilometers.

The next morning two of us, along with an MCC volunteer, headed out on bicycles from El Carmen to La Cabeza, an Indian settlement about seven kilometers away. When we arrived we were warmly greeted by a group of women who knew we were coming and were already making preparations for the noon meal. While they cooked, we visited with them and learned about how the women, with no help from the men of the village, tilled their own fields of rice and beans. After we ate together, we walked out to the fields, another couple kilometers from the village.

When I left—dead tired—on my borrowed bicycle to return to El Carmen, then to Santa Cruz, and eventually back home to the United States, I knew I would never see these women again. But I also knew that they had touched me in a way I would never forget; although our lives were very different, we shared the love of our families and cared for our children with the same intensity. My visit with them was like a delicious dessert at the end of a satisfying meal. Their hospitality, offered graciously and without pretense, left me with a wonderful and lingering sweet taste.

Desserts, shared with strangers or friends, perhaps over a steaming cup of coffee or a pot of tea, can be the means by which relationships are nurtured. Most of the time we don't really need dessert to satisfy our hunger, but we do need dessert to leave that sweet taste of hospitality celebrated.

Rice Pudding
India

Kheer
(KHEER)

Serves 4

Boil until soft in 1¹/₂ cups of water:
    1 c. white rice
Add and stir well while simmering (about 30 minutes):
    1 tin sweetened condensed milk diluted
        with 2 tins of water
    ¹/₂ c. raisins
    pistachio nuts
    1 t. anise seed
Keep mixture moist by adding milk or water.
When creamy in texture, place in bowl and garnish with slivered almonds.
Serve either cold or warm.

– Allen and Leoda Buckwalter,
Elizabethtown, PA (India)

Baked Rice Pudding
England

Serves 4-6

Put the following ingredients in a lightly greased baking dish and stir to mix:
    ¹/₂ c. rice
    ¹/₄ c. brown sugar, packed
    4 c. milk
Dot with **1 oz. butter** cut into small pieces and place in preheated oven at 300°.
Bake for 2¹/₂ hours or until the liquid is absorbed and the rice is tender. Stir once or twice during the cooking period.

– Judy Smith and June Simmonds, London, England

L eora Yoder remembers the occasion a fellow missionary requested the cook to make a particular dessert for supper. After Leora had eaten her share, her friend, suspecting something amiss, asked what the cook had used to make the dessert—only to discover it was cockroach poison. And Leora lives to tell the tale!

Flan or Custard
Venezuela

Quesillo
(Kay-SEE-yoh)

Serves 12

To carmelize sugar, brown in casserole or baking pan with lid:

¹/₄ c. white sugar

Let it brown well, tipping from side to side to coat bottom of pan.

Beat:

5 eggs

Add to beaten eggs:

1 can sweetened condensed milk
1 can fresh milk (use sweetened condensed milk can to measure)
¹/₂ t. vanilla

Pour this mixture into caramelized sugar, cover and place in a pan of boiling water on top of the stove.

Boil for about ¹/₂ hour or until the quesillo is set. To test, remove the lid and insert a knife. If the knife comes out clean, the quesillo is done. Remove from hot water. When cool, invert on a platter. The carmelized sugar which liquifies in the process keeps the quesillo from sticking to the pan. Refrigerate and serve cold.

Desserts are not commonly eaten with dinner in Venezuela but this is a typical one that might be served.

– Thata Book, Manheim, PA (Venezula)

Sometimes a visitor arriving at a homestead will announce his presence thus, "Esomhambi asinganani." It is a way of greeting like saying, "Here I am, accept my presence. I will not upset your budget."

– Doris Dube, Bulawayo, Zimbabwe

While at Madra, Zambia, I was asked to make wedding cakes. It was always the bridegroom who asked me to do this. I tried layer cakes several times, but because of the heat and transportation difficulties, I usually ended up baking a large chiffon cake and decorating it appropriately. Having only a wood stove with no thermometer for baking, it was surprising how well chiffon cakes turned out, even when all one had to cook with was either green or wet wood. In those days many brides and grooms had to walk or go by bicycle from the church to the village, so often I transported the bride and groom as well as the precious cake in my vehicle.

– Ardys E. Thuma, Bradford, OH

Persimmon Custard
Japan

Combine and pour into greased baking dish:

2 c. persimmon pulp, scooped from persimmon
$1/2$ c. sugar
2 egg yolks, slightly beaten
$1/2$ t. soda
$1/4$ t. cinnamon
$1/8$ t. nutmeg
pinch of salt

Set baking dish in pan of hot water and bake slowly, about 325° for 15 minutes.

To make meringue, beat until stiff:

2 egg whites
$1/4$ c. sugar
pinch of salt

Place meringue on top of custard and bake until slightly browned.

– Lucille Graybill, Osaka, Japan

Pumpkin Custard Pie and Cups
Pennsylvania Dutch

Serves 12

Separate **3 eggs**. Beat whites until stiff and set aside.

Beat yolks and add:

2 c. mashed pumpkin (or canned)
2 c. sugar
$^1/_4$ c. margarine or butter, melted
$^1/_2$ c. flour

Stir in:

1 qt. milk, powdered or skim

Fold in beaten egg whites.

Pour into 9-inch pastry-lined pie pan and 6 custard cups.

Sprinkle with cinnamon.

Place custard cups in a pan and add 1 inch of hot water.

Bake pie and custard cups at 400° for 10 minutes. Reduce temperature to 350° and bake 45 minutes longer.

– Mrs. Herbert Kreider, Hershey, PA

I t was Edna Lehman's cooking weekend at Sikalongo Mission. She told me she planned to make ice cream, which was news that really excited me. In order to really surprise the David Climenhaga family and me, she chose to make maraschino cherry ice cream, for she had seen, she thought, a jar of cherries on the pantry shelf.

Unfortunately, she made the ice cream with the red onions I had bought in a Livingston store. Apparently there was no time to read the label or get the whiff of the onion aroma.

That dessert was a great disappointment to all of us when we ate our first taste of the "maraschino" ice cream. We felt so sorry for the cook's efforts only to have a cooking failure!

– Anna Graybill,
Hershey, PA (Zimbabwe)

Granadilla Pudding
Zimbabwe

Serves 6

Heat in double boiler:
  2¹/₂ c. milk
Mix together in a bowl:
  1 egg, beaten
  ¹/₄ c. sugar
  3 T. cornstarch
  ¹/₄ t. salt
  ¹/₂ c. milk
Gradually stir the mixture into the hot milk.
Cook and stir until thickened.
Blend in:
  1 T. margarine
  1¹/₂ t. vanilla
Chill slightly, then add:
  4 granadilla or passion fruit, pulp only
Mix well and serve cold.

– Mildred Yoder, Bulawayo, Zimbabwe

Cindy's Wet-Bottom Shoo Fly Pie
Pennsylvania Dutch

Serves 6-8

Mix:
  1 c. flour
  ²/₃ c. brown sugar
  1 T. shortening
Set aside ¹/₂ c. of crumbs for topping.
To the remaining crumbs add the following mixture:
  1 t. soda dissolved in ³/₄ c. hot water
  1 c. molasses
  1 egg, well beaten
  1 t. vanilla
Pour into unbaked pie shell and sprinkle the ¹/₂ c. crumbs on top of pie.
Bake for 10 minutes at 425°, then 350° until brown (20-25 minutes).

– Lois Jean Peterman, Lancaster, PA

175

Plum Pudding
New Mexico

Serves 4-6

Combine all ingredients in a saucepan:
> 1 can (16 oz.) plums or 1 lb. fresh plums
> $^3/_4$ T. tapioca
> $^1/_3$ t. almond extract
> $^1/_2$ c. sugar (less if using canned plums)
> Dash of salt
> Several drops red food coloring

Bring to boil and simmer until slightly thickened. This can be served as a pudding or as a pie filling.

During our time of service at the Navajo Mission, one of the continuing challenges was working with food and preparing meals for family and guests. We had an ample supply of food but the challenges were the high altitude (about 6,000 feet) and different ingredients than what we were used to. I found this recipe in one of the kitchen cupboards and discovered it to be an ingenious way to use poor quality plums of which, at that time, we had a generous supply.

– Marilyn Smith, Souderton, PA
(Navajo Mission, New Mexico)

Rich Egg Custard
England

Serves 4

Put the following ingredients into a 1-quart baking dish and mix well:
> 4 eggs
> 3 T. sugar
> 2 c. milk

Sprinkle $^1/_2$ t. grated nutmeg over the mixture. Put baking dish into a deep baking tin, half-filled with cold water. Bake in oven preheated to 325° for 45 minutes or until set.

– Judy Smith and June Simmonds, London, England

Cassava Cake
Malawi

Serves 8

Cassava is a root and may be purchased in season in fresh food section of supermarket.

Beat:
  2 eggs
Add:
  ³/₄ c. sugar
  3 T. melted shortening or butter
  ³/₄ c. coconut milk
Add and mix well:
  1 c. fresh cassava, grated
  ¹/₂ c. young coconut (optional)
Fold in:
  4 T. grated cheese
Pour into greased 9x 9-inch pan. Bake at 350° for 40 minutes.
Brush with **1 T. butter,** then sprinkle top with a little sugar and bake for an additional 5 minutes. Continue baking until golden brown.

– Mel Andricks, Mangochi, Malawi

"The tummy of a traveller is no larger than the horn of a goat." This means that travellers should not be denied any refreshment if they should suddenly turn up unexpectedly. What they may eat would probably be so little that it would easily fit into the horn of a goat.

– Doris Dube, Bulawayo, Zimbabwe

Carrot Pudding
India

Gajar Halva
(GAH-jer HAL-vah)

Serves 8

In a heavy saucepan heat:
4 c. whole milk
Add:
1 lb. carrots, finely grated
Bring to boil and continue boiling slowly for two to three hours.
Add and continue cooking over low heat for another 1/2 hour, stirring occasionally:
1 can sweetened condensed milk
1/2 c. sugar
Add **8 T. butter** and cook for another ten minutes.
Remove from heat and stir in:
8 whole cardamoms.
Garnish with 1/4 c. sliced almonds and raisins.
Serve hot (may be slightly runny).

– Mary Roy, Bihar, India

Let's be generous in this life, knowing our true reward will be to enjoy God's perfect hospitality in our eternal home.

Don't wait for company to knock on your door. Be an inviter.

– Keith D. Wright, Evangelical Visitor, p. 6, Feb. 1996

Deluxe English Trifle
England

Serves 9-12

Bake in 2 round layers and cool:
One yellow cake mix
Cook (or use instant) and cool:
**1 6-oz. package vanilla pudding mix, using
½ c. extra milk.**

To assemble: split one layer of cake in two. Put top half on a plate. Put other half in bottom of flat-bottom glass bowl (trimmed to size of bowl). Drain:
1 20 oz. can of fruit cocktail, saving the juice.
Pour the juice over the two split layers of cake. Pour one-half of the fruit over the cake in the glass bowl. Pour one-half of the pudding over the fruit. Repeat the three layers: cake, fruit, and pudding. Cover and refrigerate several hours. Before serving spread top with **sweetened whipped cream or Cool Whip**. Decorate with **cherries or slivered almonds.**

To serve, spoon into dessert dishes at the table.

When we were in England in 1974, on Morris's sabbatical, I discovered a "box mix" for "Luxury Trifle" in the supermarket. The box had cake, pudding mix, a tin of mixed fruit, and a package of topping mix, all in one box. I cut out the directions, brought it home and adapted into our ingredients here. This is one of my favorite company desserts.

– Leone Sider, Grantham, PA

Leora Yoder remembers staff birthday celebrations she hosted at Madhipura Christian Hospital when up to 50 people shared in the birthday cake and sweet tea—except Markus who preferred salt in his tea!

Mexican Fruit Cake
Southern United States

Beat together:
  1¹/₂ c. sugar
  2 eggs
Mix together and add to egg mixture:
  2 c. flour
  2 t. baking soda
Stir in:
  1 20-oz. can crushed pineapple with juice
  1 c. chopped nuts
Bake in an ungreased 9x13-inch pan at 350° for 35 minutes.
Use mixer to mix icing:
  1 8-oz. cream cheese (low fat or regular)
  1 t. vanilla
  ¹/₂ stick margarine
Add:
  2 c. powdered sugar
Spread on cake while still warm.
Chill before serving.
This freezes well and can be served right from the freezer.

– Vanessa Rubley, McMinnville, TN

Muva Yinkosi
"He who eats last is a king."

In most homes people eat together. Sometimes they even share from the same plate. Occasionally individuals may for some reason or other eat long after everyone else has eaten. When this happens the people will say, "Muva yinkosi" (this individual is to be envied). He is enjoying his food when everyone else has long finished. Sometimes this person is also getting a little bit more than everyone else because all the dishes are to be cleaned out in readiness for the next meal. He is indeed a king!

– Doris Dube,
Bulawayo, Zimbabwe

Indian Pudding
Cree of Saskatchewan

Serves 12-16

Measure flour into a large bowl and cut in margarine:

- 4 c. flour
- $1/4$ c. margarine

Add the following ingredients:

- 2 T. baking powder
- $1/4$ t. salt
- $1/4$ t. allspice
- $1/4$ t. cinnamon
- $1/4$ c. currants
- $1/2$ c. raisins

Mix the following ingredients and add to above:

- $1/2$ c. brown sugar
- $1 1/2$ c. molasses
- $1/2$ c. white sugar
- $1/4$ t. salt
- $1/2$ c. water

Lightly grease 4 12-oz. coffee tins, cut circles of wax paper, place in bottoms of tins. Divide dough into the 4 tins. Cover tins with aluminum foil. Put large kettle (canner) on stove with rack in bottom, and add 2 inches of water. Put puddings in kettle on rack, cover and steam 3 hours. Add more boiling water if necessary. Lift from kettle, remove foil and cool for 20 minutes. Run table knife around pudding and gently shake loose and remove from tins. Cool right side up until cold. Cover with cloth while cooling. To serve, reheat pudding in oven, or microwave, or return to a coffee tin, cover and steam about 45 minutes. Serve with milk (optional).

This would be made for Christmas or New Years Day. The Indians didn't have ovens on the trapline and so by boiling, this dessert was made possible.

– Jennie Rensberry, LaLoche, SK and Leone Sider, Grantham, PA

Rosy Rhubarb
Pennsylvania Dutch

Serves 10-12

Sift together:
  2 c. flour
  ¹/₄ t. salt
  2¹/₂ t. baking powder
Then cut ¹/₂ c. **margarine** into the flour mix.
Add and work into a dough:
  1 egg, slightly beaten
  ³/₄ c. milk
Spread into greased 9x13-inch pan, bringing up around sides a bit.
Spread:
  6 c. diced rhubarb on dough.
Sprinkle:
  3 oz. red jello on top of the rhubarb.
Topping:
  6 T. margarine
  1¹/₄ c. sugar
  ¹/₂ c. flour
Crumble topping with fingers and spread on top.
Then sprinkle with 1 oz. red jello.
Bake at 350° for 30-40 minutes.

May serve with milk or ice cream, but it is delicious served plain.

– Millie Sollenberger, Hagerstown, MD

People love to eat! Food presentation doesn't need to be highly formal or extra fancy. Simply ask the Holy Spirit to bless your efforts, and bring on the food!

– Keith D. Wright, Evangelical Visitor, p. 5, Feb. 1996

Wild Cranberry Bars
Cree of Saskatchewan

Combine:
  2 c. wild (fresh or frozen) cranberries
  $^1/_4$ c. water
  1 c. sugar
Bring to a boil, stirring to prevent sticking.
Simmer 10 minutes. Mash berries.
Combine:
  $1^1/_2$ c. quick cooking rolled oats
  1 c. flour
  $^1/_4$ t. baking soda
  $^1/_2$ c. brown sugar
  $^1/_4$ t. salt
Cut into above:
  $^1/_2$ c. butter
Press $^1/_2$ of the mixture into an 8x8-inch pan.
Spread cranberry sauce over the base, and
sprinkle with remaining crumbs.

One $15^1/_2$-oz. can of regular cranberry sauce may
be used, instead of fresh or frozen cranberries.

Koonu's father is a Cree Indian and a member of
the provincial parliament.

– Koonu Goulet, Saskatchewan, Canada

You too can practice hospitality with an evangelistic thrust
by developing the attitudes of sharedness, zeal, cheerful-
ness, and generosity.

– Keith D. Wright, Evangelical Visitor, p. 6, Feb. 1996

Persimmon Bars
Japan

Mix all ingredients well:
1 c. soft persimmon pulp
1 c. sugar
1 c. flour
$^1/_2$ c. milk
$^1/_2$ t. cinnamon
$^1/_2$ t. nutmeg
2 t. baking soda
1 T. butter
pinch salt
Pour batter into 8 x 9-inch pan. Bake at 250° for 45 minutes.

Persimmons are plentiful in Japan and missionaries found many ways to use the overabundance of soft persimmons.

– Ruth Zook, Mechanicsburg, PA (Japan)

Peanut Crunches
Zimbabwe

Makes 2 Dozen

Beat until thick and lemon–colored:
1 egg
Add and mix well:
$^1/_4$ c. sugar
$^1/_8$ t. salt
Add and stir:
2 c. raw peanuts, chopped
Drop small spoonfuls on a greased cookie sheet; mash cookies flat. Bake at 350° for 15 minutes until edges begin to brown.

This recipe was used by the older missionaries when they returned from village visitation with gifts of peanuts or "monkey nuts" given in appreciation for the visits.

– Grace Holland, Ashland, Ohio(Zimbabwe)

Lemon Squares Québec

Miettes au citron
(ME-et oh SEH-trohn)

Serves 12

Lemon filling:
Mix together and heat in saucepan over medium heat until thickened (bubbles slightly):
   2 c. sugar
   2 c. water
   4 T. cornstarch
Remove from heat and add:
   2 eggs, slightly beaten
Return to heat two to three minutes. Stir constantly.
Remove from heat and cool to room temperature. Then add:
   ¹/₃ c. lemon juice (adjust to taste)
Mix the following crumb mixture:
   1³/₄ c. of plain soda crackers (unsalted), crumbled
   ³/₄ c. flour
   ³/₄ c. sugar
   1 t. baking powder
   ³/₄ c. butter (cut in with knife)
   ³/₄ c. coconut
Place half of crumb mixture in 8x8-inch pan. Spread with filling cooled to room temperature. Cover with rest of crumb mixture. Bake at 375° about 30 minutes or until coconut is golden brown.

My mother began making this dessert for us in the late 1930s and now I make it for my grandchildren. It's also a popular treat at the weekly Bible Study in my home.

– *Thérèse Baillargeon, St. Romuald, Québec*

Persimmon Cookies
Japan

Cream until fluffy:
    ¹/₂ c. softened butter or margarine
    1 c. granulated sugar
Add to above mixture and beat well:
    1 large egg
Then add and mix well:
    1 c. strained persimmon pulp
    1 t. soda
    1 t. vanilla
Sift together:
    1 c. all-purpose flour
    1 t. cinnamon
    1 t. nutmeg
    ¹/₂ t. salt
Add the following to the flour mixture:
    1 c. raisins, chopped
    1 c. nuts, chopped
Combine mixtures and mix well. Drop by
teaspoonfuls onto greased baking sheets and bake
at 350° for 12 minutes.

– Lucille Graybill, Osaka, Japan

Full stomach, happy heart.

– Colombian proverb

Fatty Cookies
Zimbabwe

2 dozen

Combine in mixing bowl:
1 egg, well beaten
1¹/₂ T. sugar
1¹/₄ c. milk
Add and stir until smooth:
2 c. flour
3 t. baking powder
¹/₂ t. salt
Heat **1 t. oil** in frying pan. Drop batter by small
spoonfuls into the pan. Fry like small pancakes.
Cookies may be spread with jam and served
with tea.

For most African people, this is a popular accompaniment with tea. I remember my mother, not
very experienced in cooking the fatty cookies,
would time and again forget to add either the salt
or the sugar. I would remind her each time she
made these cookies, "Don't forget the salt which
you forgot the last time." She would then remember the salt and forget the sugar. It became a
family joke in our home.

– Jester Mlilo, Bulawayo, Zimbabwe

"**H**ands wash each other" (one good
turn deserves another).
Mrs. Ncube may do a good
turn for Mrs. Nyoni. At a
later date when Mrs.
Ncube has even forgotten
about what she did, Mrs.
Nyoni may surprise her by
performing a kindness
towards her. Mrs. Ncube
may protest and say, "You
really shouldn't have
bothered," and Mrs. Nyoni
will respond, "Izandle ziya
gezana."

– Doris Dube,
Bulawayo, Zimbabwe

The Community Calabaza Party

Five weeks after we were married, my husband John and I became missionaries to Cuba. We lived in a beautiful little stucco house with a tiny yard in front and a fruitful patio in back (coconut palms, tangerine tree, papaya tree). Although the accepted method of mowing the lawn was to hoe everything out, John did occasionally see a tuft of grass or other plant he wanted to encourage to grow. When a particular plant grew recognizable as a calabaza (squash) plant, we watched to see what would come of it. The neighbor children also saw it and one by one declared that they were not responsible for that plant in our yard. Well, the plant grew and grew and vined all over our little yard, and began to get calabazas on it–not just one or two, but many. Then the neighborhood children began to claim that they were the ones who had cast the seed into the yard.

Now here was a dilemma. Although there were many calabazas, there were even more children, and we had been carefully taught that we should not show partiality among the people. There were more squash than we would use, but it would not do to give calabazas to some and not to all. Finally I went to a mother who attended the church and had children in our school. I asked her if she would please tell me how to make "flan de calabaza," a squash custard something like the filling of a pumpkin pie. Yes, she could tell me, and proceeded something like this:

Cook and mash the **calabaza.**
Add some milk, and stir in **a couple eggs.**
Put in a **pinch of salt**, a small handful of **cinnamon**, and **sugar** to sweeten.
Mix it all together and bake.

I was grateful for the information as far as it went, but as a newlywed, I did not feel confident to proceed. However, we took the risk, and sent word all up and down the street that at a certain hour on a certain day all the children should come to our house. The flan did thicken properly, and as the children gathered (more than forty, if I remember correctly), we put squares of flan on square "plates" of aluminum foil, and handed them around to the excited children. Let it never be said the missionaries were either partial or selfish!

If you want to make your own flan, I would recommend looking up a pumpkin pie filling recipe in your favorite cookbook. (The recipe for Venezuelan flan on page 172 is a "company" version of this dish. Ed.)

– *Ruth Pawelski, Dayton, OH (Cuba)*

Special

"I was a stranger
and you invited
me in."

—Matthew 25:35

In the middle of a series of parables in Matthew about judgment and the end times is the parable of the sheep and the goats. Whatever else it is intended to teach, it is a call to hospitality—to offer food and water to the hungry and thirsty, visit prisoners, provide clothing to those who don't have any, and invite strangers home. As Edith Schaeffer, in *Hidden Art*, asserts, "When we are told to be 'given to hospitality,' it [doesn't mean] that we are to be hospitable only to old friends" (Wheaton, IL: Tyndale House, p.128).

That theme was echoed by Terry Brensinger, Old Testament professor at Messiah College, in his 1997 Susquehanna Conference sermon on "Being an Everywhere Missionary." He defined hospitality as the "extension of life to those to whom we have no formal responsibility," and noted that it is also an "antidote to preoccupation with ourselves" and an opportunity reach out "beyond our comfort zones" to those who need the kind of intimacy between people that true hospitality affords.

He went on to describe an experience of hospitality received when he was living in Jordan. Upon hitchhiking a ride with a Jordanian truck driver, he was invited to the man's home for a cup of tea enroute to another destination, and then he was invited for supper and to spend the night. The truck driver's entire extended family came to welcome the stranger. A similar example of Middle Eastern hospitality is described in an article called *Land of a Thousand and One Courtesies*. In Iran, the subject of the article, "strangers are invariably surprised by the ceremonial that unfolds before them on a visit to an Iranian household....To enter someone's house is like coming to the end of a journey through the dust of the desert and slaking one's thirst in a garden" (Yann Richard in *UNESCO Courier*, February 1990, p. 30).

In the midst of severe drought in Zambia in 1992, Bishop Enock Shamapani and his wife Lastinah opened their home to two visitors from the United States and served a generous traditional Zambian meal. When the visitors talked with him later about the pressures created by drought conditions, Bishop Shamapani confessed that sometimes he and his wife really didn't have enough food to share, but they were compelled to do so anyway because hospitality is so deeply ingrained in Zambian culture. Besides, he couldn't stop thinking about Jesus' words,

"When you did it for the least of these brothers and sisters of mine, you did it for me."

In urban America, an older woman lived by herself for a time in a public housing project. Those who lived in the projects understood the unwritten rules and hierarchy of life in the projects. There was also an element of danger and risk, and therefore it was generally accepted that one did not open one's home to strangers. But Mrs. Neal wasn't one to adapt to what was generally accepted. Despite the taboos and dangers associated with doing so, she frequently offered coffee and sandwiches to transient and homeless people who came through the projects. When her granddaughter would stop by while she was serving someone and express concern about what she was doing, Mrs. Neal would answer, "Why would I refuse to help? Look at him! He needs food. Besides, he might be Jesus!" Recently, Mrs. Neal died at age 89. Her granddaughter spoke at her funeral of the legacy she left behind for her family and friends.

What a wonderful legacy for us all—to be remembered and emulated as people who saw Jesus in everyone and freely offered our hospitality to strangers and friends, poor and rich, neighbors and foreigners, young and old.

"I was a stranger and you took me in," said Jesus.

Planning an Indian Dinner Celebration

The Carlisle Brethren in Christ Church Missions and Service Committee decided to highlight the conclusion of a mission's project with a celebration dinner.

The meal came together as a joint effort of the Missions and Service Committee. One member of the committee was familiar with the food and its preparation. This person served as the coordinator for the events. Preparation events included: deciding the menu, multiplying the recipes to prepare for the appropriate number of guests, and making a trip to purchase the needed items.

With everything on hand the committee met for a regular monthly meeting, took care of business items, and then went to the church kitchen to begin preparation. This was a Thursday evening and the meal was to be served Sunday evening.

Many recipes called for chopping or slicing onions and other ingredients. The first evening was spent working on these preparations. We could make the items that were to be served cold. We also began work on other items, such as hard-boiling eggs for a curry, and making the meat balls for another curry.

Our next time together was Saturday morning. Some people shredded cabbage, others peeled hard-boiled eggs while others washed potatoes. Still others chopped onions until, one by one, each curry was made. We began with the egg curry, then the meat ball curry, and finally finished with the cabbage curry.

Each dish gets tastier the longer it stands. Because of this, making them the day before is not a problem. When we gathered Sunday afternoon to finish our work, the curries just needed heating. We made large quantities of rice in the cooking pans of two roaster ovens which worked quite well. When it was time to serve the meal we served the plates directly from the cooking pots and pans. This is often done in large feast settings in Northern India.

One other preparation the committee made for this event was to dress in Indian outfits and to decorate the room with items from India available to us. We were privileged to have a retired missionary from India as our guest speaker for the evening. It was a pleasure to be able to bring a feeling of another country into our experience during this celebration event.

– Ken Hoke, Carlisle, PA

Special

Recipes
for an Indian Dinner for 50 as served at Carlisle Brethren in Christ Church Under direction of Pastor Ken Hoke

Menu for an Indian Dinner to serve 50

Rice
Egg Curry
Beef Kofta Curry (Meat Ball Curry)
Cabbage Curry
Raita
Orange Chutney

Rice

Cook as per package instructions. Long grain rice is preferred.
If you use Indian Basmati rice, estimate $1/4$ cup rice per person (1 cup rice to $1^3/4$ cups water).

Stove top: Bring cold water and rice to hard boil. Turn heat to very low. Cover and cook without stirring until water is absorbed. Turn heat off. Leaving lid on, allow rice to steam and fluff 10–20 minutes longer, depending on amount of rice.

Oven: Bake water and rice at 350°. Length of time depends on amount of rice.

Egg Curry

Hard boil, peel and cut in half lengthwise:
>   5 $^1/_2$ doz. eggs

In 1 c. vegetable oil, sauté until onions are golden:
>   16 medium onions, minced
>   2 T. and 2 t. marjoram
>   2 T. and 2 t. thyme
> $^1/_2$ c. parsley flakes

Add and cook lightly for 2 to 3 minutes:
>   2 T. and 2 t. turmeric
> $^1/_3$ c. salt
>   5 T. and 1 t. dried, unsweetened coconut
> $^1/_2$ c. curry powder

Add and stir very carefully so as not to break the eggs:
>   hard boiled eggs
>   32 large tomatoes, chopped
>   4 pt. plain yogurt

Cover the pan, lower heat, and allow to simmer for 10 minutes.

Beef Kofta (meat ball) Curry

Serves 50

Blend together the following:
>   6 med.onions, minced
>   36 cloves garlic, minced
>   6 T. Worcestershire sauce
> $^1/_4$ c. marjoram
>   2 T. thyme
>   3 T. salt
>   6 T. curry powder
>   6 beaten eggs

Add above mixture to:
>   6 lb. ground beef

Shape into balls of desired size and fry slowly.

While these meatballs can be used for hors d'oeuvres, as a side dish with curries, or for snacks, they can also be prepared as a curry.

(continued on next page)

Beef Kofta Curry
(continued)

To curry the meat balls:
Sauté in 6 T. oil:
  6 onions, chopped
  2 T. ground ginger
Add and cook 5 minutes:
  2 T. turmeric
  2 T. curry powder
  1 T. salt
Add and stir to coat:
  24 med. potatoes, cubed
Then add and cook well for 5-10 minutes:
  3 lb. tomatoes, sliced
  6 T. yogurt or lemon juice
Add meat balls and cover with:
  3 qt. hot water
Simmer, stirring occasionally, until potatoes are tender.

Cabbage Curry

Serves 50

Sauté until golden in ³/₄ c. butter or vegetable oil:
  8 small onions, thinly sliced
  2 T. ground ginger
Add and mix well:
  2 T. and 2 t. turmeric
  5 T. salt
  1 T. and 1 t. black pepper
Add and cook uncovered for 15 minutes:
  16 lbs. firm white cabbage, shredded
    coarsely
Add, cover and cook until excess liquid is absorbed (about 1 hour):
  2 T. and 2 t. lemon juice
Uncover, add and sauté until thoroughly dry:
  ¹/₂ c. vegetable oil
Add and continue to cook for 5 minutes:
  5 T. and 1 t. curry powder
  Salt to taste and serve.

Raita

(about 4 cups)

Peel, grate and set aside for one hour:
  12 medium cucumbers
Mix together:
  6 medium onions, minced
  1 T. ground cumin
  6 pt. yogurt
  2 t. salt
Drain all water from cucumber and add to the yogurt mixture. Serve as a side dish to curry.

Orange Chutney

(about 4 cups)

Mix together:
  24 oranges, peeled, diced and seeded
  6 medium onions, minced
  3 c. grated coconut
  6 T. mint leaves, crushed
Cover and chill in refrigerator. Serve as a side dish to curry.

Then Jacob gave Esau some bread and some lentil stew. He ate and drank, and then got up and left.

– Genesis 25:34

In many Indian homes the main meal consists of rice or chappatis served with lentils or a vegetable curry.

Rice and lentils are often cooked together to make Dal Kitcherie. Onions are browned in a little oil. Salt and pepper, and a touch of red pepper, if available, are added along with the lentils and rice and all cooked until soft and thick. When evening comes, the husband and children eat first and the wife often eats alone when everyone else is finished. Food is served on brass plates with tin or colorful enamel plates for the children.

Chappatis are round, flat Indian bread made from whole wheat flour. To 1 cup flour and $1/2$ teaspoon salt, add water gradually to moisten (similar to baking powder biscuit dough). Knead for five minutes until somewhat elastic. Set aside for 30 minutes if you have time before the meal. Shape dough into six balls and roll out to a five-inch diameter with rolling pin on flat, floured surface. Heat a non–stick frying pan until very hot and fry the chappatis on both sides, holding down gently around edges with a small clean cloth or a pancake turner until slightly brown. Then press carefully in center to puff the chappati. While the chappati is frying, a delightful aroma fills the house. Serve hot with a vegetable curry or as a bread with a simple soup.

In 480 AD Benedict said, "People enter our lives to enrich us by their differences, and to be graciously received in the name of Christ."

More Specials

Ham Loaf
Pennsylvania Dutch

Serves 100

Mix:
   13 lb. lean ground ham
   13 lb. lean ground fresh pork
   9³/₄ c. rolled crackers (saltines)
   2 c. chopped onions
   2¹/₂ doz. eggs
   13 c. milk
   1 c. chopped parsley
Shape into 13 loaves - 9x5x3 inches.
Mix:
   3 lb. brown sugar
   3 c. vinegar
   ¹/₂ c. dry mustard
Boil 1 minute.
Baste the loaves while baking at 350° for
1¹/₂ hours.

Note from recipe donor, Anna Ruth Ressler: In the
early 1960s this recipe was served at a Franklin
County Missions Conference held at the Antrim
Brethren in Christ Church.
(I received this recipe from Martha Wingert at
that time and have used it ever since with some
adaptations.)

– Martha Wingert, Franklin County, Pennsylvania

When you are hungry, even the most tasteless fruit tastes like
your favorite dessert.

– Indian proverb

Chicken for the Bride and Groom
Zambia

1 stewing chicken
water to cover
2 t. salt

Kill, dress, and clean the chicken. Wash carefully. Remove only the chicken's feet. Do NOT cut in pieces. The chicken should be cooked whole in a medium-sized pot. Cover with water, add salt and cook.

Beliefs:

1. Cooking the chicken whole represents the building of the house (marriage and family).
2. Removing the legs: chickens usually scratch around in the dirt and destroy things. Leaving the legs would symbolize the destruction of the house (family, marriage), so the legs are removed to prevent such destruction. Also, the chicken's feet are commonly eaten here, but the women are discouraged from eating them as it is thought that they will go "scratching about" and cause problems and destruction. The back of the chicken is reserved for the head of the household.

– Esther Kalambo, Macha Hospital, Choma, Zambia

The Lord's Supper affords us an extraordinary menu: Jesus himself. In offering the bread and the wine, Jesus said, "This is my body . . . .. This is my blood."

– Unknown

199

Curried
Meat Dish
Malawi

Njama ya Kare
(Ku-ree)

2-4 lb. meat (beef, chicken)
2-10 lb. cornmeal - specially treated
Curry used in most cases is directly plucked from a tree
1 t.- 1 T. salt
1/3 c. cooking oil for lean meat

The method here is difficult to describe since the curry is prepared by a group of women, each cook striving to do her best so as to out-shine her mates. With the appropriate ingredients the preparation varies. In a village setting measurement and cooking temperature vary.

The curry is served three times: first, as soon as the dish is ready, then as the mid-day meal, and last the meal is served in the village setting where one is free to sample all the foods and the day is crowned by celebrating.

Masanje is a festive occasion with the main dishes being dry beans and meat (pork, beef, or chicken). Therefore, the ingredients vary as it is a group occasion. This is both a celebration and a show. The festival is held along the bank of a river with natural beauty and clean water.

– Enesi Zulu, Diwiza Village, and
Rev. E.B. Disi, Blantyre, Malawi

A Traditional
Recipe
Zambia

In a large pot of boiling water add **corn meal** and cook until soft, as if making porridge. While the porridge is cooking, in another pot cook **a root** in water after pounding it to a pulp. Boil for 30 minutes. Strain the liquid from the root and add to the porridge. Cook and serve with sugar.

– Mrs. L. Hamaseele,
pastor's wife,
Macha Brethren in Christ
Church, Choma, Zambia

Preparations for a Christmas Party

On the day before Christmas I pound some **corn** (maize) into **grits** (mealie rice), preparing it nicely so my children will enjoy it. I wash the grits and put it in a pot. Then I cover it with water and boil it. While it is boiling I pound **raw peanuts** (groundnuts) and add these to the grits when it is soft. Then I stir all together and cook over low heat until the peanuts have cooked, and the contents in the pot have thickened. This is called *Samp*. (2 cups grits, water to cover, adding more as needed, 2 cups pounded peanuts. Serve with sugar added as desired). I also prepare dried vegetables and I put them in the pot to cook with added salt. When they are cooked and most of the water has boiled away, I add pounded peanuts and cook this relish until it is done. This is what we prepare for this special day. When the food is ready I call the children to eat. It is a really nice way to celebrate.

– Bina Jay and Mrs. E. Moyo, Macha Hospital Choma, Zambia

Lord Jesus, please make us more loving and giving–help us to think what we can do for the hungry, and give us the determination to do it. In Jesus name, Amen.

– 365 Children's Prayers, written and compiled by Carol Watson, 1989, Lion Publishing P.C., Sandy Lane West, Little More, Oxford, England

Outdoor Fresh Fish Fry

(By fresh we mean less than ten minutes from the lake to the pan!)

We don't have the usual fare of entertainment because we live so far north, so we do other things like going fishing and frying our catch on a fire on a sandy shore.

Catch twice as many fish as you think you will need because you may work up an amazing appetite in the great outdoors.

Find a sandy shore on the lake and beach the boat. All hands on deck needed to pull the boat up on the sand.

Divide into three groups for the following jobs:
Clean and fillet the fish.
Gather dry twigs and branches to make a small hot fire.
Get the food box and set up a wilderness kitchen.

While the lard is heating in a cast iron skillet, dip the fillets in flour, add salt and pepper, then fry on both sides until golden and crisp. Say a prayer of thanksgiving, find a rock or log to sit on, then enjoy the treat.

When everyone has eaten all the fish they can, each goes to find a bannock stick. Someone mixes up a batch of bannock dough:
3 c. biscuit mix
$^2/_3$ c. water

Mix and knead as best you can on the lid of the food box.

Pinch off a gob of dough the size of a golf ball. Wrap it around the end of the stick. Slowly roast over coals until the bannock is golden brown. If you bake it too fast it burns on the outside but is still uncooked on the inside.

Pull the baked bannock off the stick and stuff with butter or jam. Repeat the process until you are full or your patience has run out.

Go home with smoky hair, a full tummy, and a happy heart, praising the Lord that you don't have to eat store–bought fish sticks.

– Jennie Rensberry, La Loche, SK

Their Poverty Welled up in Generosity

In December 1992, a video producer and I went to Zambia to help document for the church in North America how the Brethren in Christ Church in Zambia had dealt with what had been called "the worst drought of the century." Although the new rainy season was just beginning and hope was strong for a good harvest, the people of Zambia were still coping with food shortages and uncertainty about the future.

As we visited villages around Macha and Sikalongo Missions to film and interview for an MCC video, we were keenly aware that our hosts had very little. Yet, in village after village, we were offered a meal and warm hospitality. We heard stories of struggle, including how the church leaders and their families shared what little they had with others in need, not knowing whether they would have enough for themselves.

We were honored and humbled by the generosity of the Zambian people as they extended their hospitality to their guests from North America. In one village where we were served goat meat with our insima (a real treat during a time of drought when meat was scarce), the headman told me he had named one of his sons after my father who had served as a missionary at Sikalongo many years before.

The Zambians we met were like the people of the Macedonian churches that Paul describes in 2 Corinthians 8:2-3: "Out of the most severe trial, their overflowing joy and their extreme poverty welled up in rich generosity. . .. They gave as much as they were able, and even beyond their ability."

– Harriet Sider Bicksler, Mechanicsburg, PA
(Missionary kid, 1948-1961 Zambia/Zimbabwe)

We always need to remember that the normal main meal for many Brethren in Christ around the world is rice, beans or bread served with one other item, probably a simply prepared vegetable. The following menus could be used for special guest meals or church fellowship meals.

Africa

Peanut Soup (Zambia), 23
Spinach and Rice Pondo (Zaire), 161
Rice and Raisin Salad (South Africa), 40
Baked Stuffed Zucchini (Egypt), 165
Cassava Cake (Malawi), 177

England

Egg and Lemon Soup, 22
Toad-in-the-Hole, 114
Steamed vegetables of choice
Deluxe English Trifle, 179
Tea or coffee

Special

India

Menu 1
Vegetable Fritters (appetizer), 31
Steamed Rice, 157
Cabbage and Pea Curry, 61
Beef Curry, 76
Fresh Tomato Chutney, 41
Rice Pudding (second course), 171

Menu 2
Cauliflour and Potato Curry, 61
Chicken Curry, 94
Vegetable Pulao, 55
Tomato Sauce, 65
Yogurt (purchased locally)
Fresh Fruit Bowl (second course)

Japan

Menu 1
Teppanyaki (Pan Sautéed Meat and Vegetables), 87
Pumpkin Cabbage Salad, 39
Fresh fruit such as Mandarin oranges
Green Tea

Menu 2
Chicken and Vegetables
    Cooked in Broth (Mizutaki), 100
Scrambled Tofu on Rice, 167
Persimmon Bars, 184
Green Tea

Latin America **Menu 1**
Pepian, 168
Creamed Potatoes, 68
    or rice, 157
Cabbage Slaw, 38

Latin America
(continued)

Menu 2
Pork Chops in Tomato Sauce, 116
Creamed Potatoes, 68
        or Rice, 157
Tamaulipeca Salad, 37

Pennsylvania Dutch

Ham Loaf, 116
German Hot Potato Salad, 152
Cooked Dried Corn, 67
Cabbage Slaw, 38
Grandma Lilley's Sweet Red Beets, 46
Cindy's Wet-Bottom Shoo Fly Pie, 175

Zambia

Tonga Chicken, 101
Cornmeal Porridge, 154
Cabbage Peanut Relish, 57
Roasted Peanuts, 28

Zimbabwe

Zimbabwe Stew, 90
Cornmeal Porridge (Sadza), 155
Peanut Butter Gravy, 140
Granadilla Pudding, 175
Peanut Crunches, 184

GEOGRAPHICAL INDEX

RECIPE INDEX